President Reagan's Conservative Fiscal Policy

Unemployment Among African Americans

Chiazam Ugo Okoye

UNIVERSITY PRESS OF AMERICA,® INC.
Lanham • Boulder • New York • Toronto • Oxford

Copyright © 2006 by
University Press of America,® Inc.
4501 Forbes Boulevard
Suite 200
Lanham, Maryland 20706
UPA Acquisitions Department (301) 459-3366

PO Box 317
Oxford
OX2 9RU, UK

Library of Congress Control Number: 2005937430
ISBN-13: 978-0-7618-3099-3 (clothbound : alk. ppr.)
ISBN-10: 0-7618-3099-5 (clothbound : alk. ppr.)
ISBN-13: 978-0-7618-3100-6 (paperback : alk. ppr.)
ISBN-10: 0-7618-3100-2 (paperback : alk. ppr.)

To
My mother and in memory of my father and their passion for education.

Table of Contents

List of Tables

Acknowledgments

I would like to express my deep appreciation and gratitude to people whose contributions made it possible for me to arrive to this stage in my quest for knowledge. First, my parents, who taught me that faith, hard-work, determination, and perseverance, could overcome any obstacle. I am indebted to my mentor, Professor Charles Harris, for his suggestions, inspiration, encouragement, and precision guidance, which were very instrumental in the conceptualization, development and successful completion of this book.

Furthermore, my deepest gratitude and appreciation goes to the entire members of Okoye family for providing the strength, inspiration, and support needed to succeed in the painstaking and frustrating process of completing a book.

Abstract

The main objective of this book is to explain the Reagan administration's fiscal policy and its impact on the level of unemployment among African Americans. Reagan's fiscal policy, based on his personal style of leadership and conservative ideology, changed the national economy and had a significant impact on the level of unemployment among African Americans. Reagan administration's fiscal policy contributed to the high level of unemployment among African Americans in the 1980s. Reaganomics and the supply-side fiscal policies produced several major budget cuts in the area of domestic employment training programs, such as the Comprehensive Employment and Training Act (CETA) Program. Several tax relief acts were passed by Congress with the influence of President Reagan. The book examines three such tax laws, they are the following: The Economic Recovery and Tax Act, 1981 (ERTA), The Tax Equity and Fiscal Responsibility Act, 1982 (TEFRA), and the Tax Reform Act of 1986 (TRA). This study examines the two terms of President Reagan's administration, from 1981 to 1988. The core of the study focuses on the Reagan administration's budget and tax policies as they relate to the unemployment of African Americans during the 1980s.

Chapter One

Introduction

Unemployment has been a potent and controversial political issue since the Great Depression of the 1930s. In the early part of 1900s political leaders treated the dangers of widespread unemployment or the plight of the jobless in a casual fashion. The Great Depression sparked a political revolution, which made presidents, and other policy makers know that the ups and downs of the unemployment rate are the most visible sign of the economy's well-being and could determine whether a politician wins or loses an election.

The United States government annually allocates billions of dollars to assist the unemployed in job-creating and training programs. Yet, there are still strong ideological divisions among policy-makers about how and when the government should attempt to solve the unemployment problem. The persistent double-digit unemployment rate among certain groups in the population ignited public fears and fostered higher demand for government intervention policies. Unemployment is one of the most hotly debated issues on the national policy agenda.

Scholars will continue to debate the lasting impact of President Ronald Wilson Reagan's administration fiscal policy for a long time. The era of the modern president begun with Franklin D. Roosevelt and more government intervention policies, and ended with Ronald W. Reagan and less government involvement in domestic economic issues. Reagan's presidency was characterized by popularity, ideology, influence, initiative, and by symbolic and pragmatic leadership. Like or hate his policies, his presence in office was one that many Americans loved.

The impact of Ronald Reagan's fiscal policy cannot be overemphasized. During President Reagan's two terms in office, he proposed major reforms in domestic economic policies. With his personality and style, he persuaded Congress to adopt many of these policies. These were known as supply-side

1

policies, and was coined "Reaganomics" by the mass-media. His policies brought significant reductions in domestic economic programs and substantial cuts in both the marginal and average tax rates for affluent taxpayers. The administration's justification for such reform policies was based on the expectation that tax breaks that are beneficial to the rich, would spur a rise in private investment, entrepreneur-ship, and the creation of jobs.

The Reagan administration's supply-side theory is probably responsible for a modest increase in the labor supply, but it did not perform a supply-side miracle for all.

The overall long-term level of unemployment is often as a result of government policies. The victims of these well-intentioned government supply-side policies are mostly poor minorities, not the more affluent, educated, highly skilled middle classes. Franklin D. Roosevelt once said, "Economic laws are not made by nature . . . but by human beings. We must fix responsibility for unemployment, runaway inflation and recurring recessions on someone for the policies causing these effects."[1]

Can government provide employment for everyone who needs it? That may be regarded as a rhetorical frivolous question since the rate of unemployment is still very high. There is a need for full employment. Unemployment leads to crime, despair, hopelessness, and more people on welfare. Many young people in the United States have no hope for the future. Older workers and disabled workers are having a hard time finding jobs while younger and able-bodied workers are being rejected. African Americans, Native Americans, Latinos, and the poor are suffering from endemic unemployment and massive lay-offs. Single mothers cannot find affordable day-care or afford the cost of transportation for each job if they want to join the labor force. Public school teachers are being laid off because of declining enrollment. Budget cuts led to civil servants being laid off. These are just a few of the problems giving rise to unemployment.

William Wilson argues that the cause of the catastrophic descent of American inner cities into increasing poverty and misery is the disappearance of work. He stated, "Work is not simply a way to make a living and support your family. It also constitutes a framework for daily behavior because it imposes discipline."[2]

The irony of it all is that there are plenty of jobs to be done in this country and yet people are out of work. There is a need to build and repair roads, bridges, water mains, and sewers, to provide urban and rural transportation and to build other physical infrastructure. There is a need for services for the disabled, the aged, and children. There is also a need for low-and middle-income housing, for healthcare and education. Policy choice can determine the level of unemployment. The need for full employment cannot be viewed in isolation from other issues that deteriorated under the Reagan administration.

The first attempt to introduce a full employment act in Congress was in 1935, but the business community defeated the measure. Later came the Full Employment Bill in 1945, and then followed the Humphrey-Hawkins Act of 1978. The objective of the bill was clearly stated: to provide jobs for everyone who wanted to work, but there was no effective means of achieving the policy objectives. Chisman points out, "We are left with a system of public policy and set of social values that are based on the assumption that virtually all Americans can and do hold good jobs, when this is clearly not the case."[3]

Jobs have become less and less secured in the last decade and if we want to hold on to our jobs, the things we have to do to keep them are becoming more difficult. Workers need to develop a high level of skills and protect themselves from a wide variety of threats to their employment conditions, their benefits, wages and promotions. George Johnson's opinion is that full employment is difficult, but that does not mean that we should ignore it.[4] Minorities face a more serious threat to their jobs, since most minorities are relatively new in the high-skilled job market and the high cost of acquiring the necessary skills is pricing poor people out of the employment market.

Another problem of skill and the availability of jobs is that up to some Americans read at or just above the elementary grade level. Most of the jobs are available to workers who can read, write, and compute at better than fifth grade level. It is unrealistic for government to expect private industry to train workers and provide them with these basic skills of reading, writing and computing. Government involvement in a full employment training program will help workers acquire the basic skills they need for employment. Education is a factor affecting the pattern of labor force participation, as well as an indicator of the quality of the labor pool.

This book focuses on the dynamic relationship between the Reagan administration's conservative fiscal policy and its impact on the level of unemployment among African Americans. It illuminates the profound effect public law and politics have on the economic well-being and employment of a selected group.

The Reagan administration's fiscal policy represented the most dramatic shift of national priorities since the FDR. The budget for social programs was severely reduced, which drastically reduced investment in job creating areas such as the railroads, housing, mass transit and safe energy production. These policies brought about particular hardships on African Americans. Congressman Hawkins provided an authoritative point of view:

> Evidence abounds that the level of unemployment we suffer and the high prices we pay are not the result of natural economic laws but stem from a deliberate choice of policies by the administration in power. Whenever an administration

truly believed in a full employment policy and really wanted to reduce unemployment as well as inflation, it was done.[5]

The average unemployment rate during the Reagan years was higher than the
rate during any other post World War II administration. The average unemployment rate for the month of March was 6.1 percent from 1968 through 1980,
but the average from 1981 through 1988 was 8.0 percent.[6] This evidence of the
high unemployment rate of the 1980s is attributed to the Reagan administration's fiscal policy. The higher unemployment rate offset the supply-side tax
benefit that was supposed to stimulate economy growth.

President Reagan stated several times that he created more jobs and that
more Americans were working than ever before. He failed to admit that 15
million people were unemployed during his presidency and that, from 1981
through 1988, 11 million people lost their jobs because of plant closings.[7]

The main significance of this research is to show how the Reagan administration's fiscal policy, shaped by his personal style of leadership and conservative ideological beliefs, changed the economy and its impact on the level
of unemployment among African Americans. Examination of this unemployment problem will help scholars; researchers and policymakers understand
more about the problem of joblessness among African Americans. The intent
of this investigation is to fill a research gap in the existing literature on unemployment problems.

This book will fill a research gap in the area of political leadership, focusing on conservative ideological public policy, and the intended or unintended
consequences of such policy for those who are politically weak and disadvantaged. Economists have studied the impact of the Reagan Administration's fiscal policy as it relates to the economy in general, and that a breakdown in terms of the level of unemployment among African Americans will
fill a vital research gap.

The general database out there was collected, verified and analyzed to
show the breakdown on the level of unemployment among African Americans. The impact of the Reagan Administration's fiscal policy on the level of
unemployment among African Americans is a unique study because most of
the existing literature examines the broader impacts.

The vast majority of research done on the problems of unemployment is by
economists. From a political point of view, the main concentration of this research is from the perspective of a policy-oriented political scientist. Therefore, the primary focus of this study is to analyze the Reagan administration's
conservative fiscal policy on unemployment and reveal the effect of such policy on the level of unemployment on African Americans.

This study is timely because there is a need to understand how and when
the government can best help the unemployed. The issue of jobs is one of the

top questions on the American agenda today. The question still remains, what can we do to attain full employment? Although the research will concentrate on a small segment of the population, an analysis of problems created by these policies will help us understand the problems facing the broader system.

There is a need to investigate the impact of fiscal policy on domestic programs. In order to understand the goals and objectives of the Reagan administration, we have to take a critical look at Reagan's fiscal policy priorities. Analyzing the impact of the Reagan administration's fiscal policy will enable us to understand the relationship between public policy formulation and implementation. An understanding of the policy making process is key in determining and assessing the implications of conservative fiscal policy impacts on African Americans in particular and on the economy in general.

Reagan, through budget and tax policies, drastically altered domestic programs. The 1980s is one of the most volatile decades in American tax reform history. Public policies are usually incremental, but the eighties were characterized by significant adjustments. The income tax cut resulted in the only decrease in federal tax receipts since the Great Depression. The formulation, implementation and impact of these policies deserve thorough examination.

It is equally important, however, to understand the social, political, and economic implications of the unemployment problem. Since we live in a system that is intertwined, such an examination is deemed necessary to add to the existing body of knowledge which helps to improve our lives.

Reagan came to office with a revolutionary agenda to set a new course in public policy. Concerning the program for economic recovery, President Reagan stated:

> My economic program is based on the fundamental precept that government must respect, protect, and enhance the freedom and integrity of the individual. My program, a careful combination of reducing incentive-stifling taxes, slowing the growth of federal spending and regulations, and a gradual slowing of the expansion of the monetary supply seeks to create a new environment in which the strengths of America can be put to work for the benefit of us all.[8]

The unemployment problems of African Americans and the poor should be of great concern to everyone. Investigating these problems and issues will increase our knowledge of the economic, social and political conditions of these groups. One of the fundamental arguments put forth by the Reagan administration was that robust economic growth is good for everyone. The administration's social welfare policy assumed that the viable economy in which the growth trickled down could provide jobs for all, along with an equitable distribution of income. The question however is the following: "How well does this premise agree with reality? To what extent does a rising tide lift all boats?"[9] This research will give us insight into the impact of the so called trickle-down policy.

NOTES

1. Augustus F. Hawkins, *"Minorities and Unemployment,"* in *What Reagan is Doing to Us?* ed. Alan Gartner et al(New York: Harper and Row, 1982), 125.

2. William Wilson, "Work," *New York Times Magazine* (August 18, 1996): 28.

3. Forrest Chisman, "An Effective Employment Policy: The Missing Middle," in *Rethinking Employment Policy,* ed. Lee Bawden and Felicity Skidmore (Washington, D.C.: Urban Institute, 1989): 251.

4. George E. Johnson, "Do We Know Enough About the Unemployment Problem to Know What, If Anything, Will Help?" in *Rethinking Employment Policy* ed. Lee Bawden and Felicity Skidmore (Washington, D.C.: Urban Institute, 1989).

5. Hawkins, "Minorities and Unemployment," 127.

6. Anandi P. Sahu and Ronald L. Tracy, *The Economic Legacy of the Reagan Years: Euphoria or Chaos?* (New York: Praeger, 1991), 62.

7. T. Varghese Kozhimannil, *The Reagan Presidency: Promises and Performances* (New York: Cimothas, 1989).

8. White House, *Program for Economic Recovery* (Washington, DC: White House, 1981), 133.

9. William Gorham, "Overview", in *The Social Contract Revisited,* ed. Lee Bawden (Washington, D.C.: Urban Institute Press, 1984).

Chapter Two

Reagan's Conservative Political Ideology, Agenda, and Strategy

President Reagan enjoyed more popularity than any other American president since Franklin Roosevelt. His popularity was partly as a result of the president's charm, good looks, humor, and strong patriotic feeling for country. He was dubbed a great communicator. These attributes have their origins in Reagan's early years. He was born Ronald Wilson Reagan, in Tampico, Illinois on February 6, 1911. His attraction was a combination of Protestant ethics, small town boy and famous movie star. The association between his leadership style and ideology is not coincidental but rather there is a strong relationship between his beliefs, his style, and his personality.

Reagan's public policies were based largely on his conservative viewpoints. This conservative rhetoric was not derived from any set of coherent existing ideology but from his conservative beliefs. These beliefs were rooted in conservative political principles, coupled with what he perceived to be a pragmatic and common-sense approach to contemporary problems. The strength of Reagan was that he simplified issues whether it was welfare reforms, the environment, spread of communism, social unrest, or national security. Reagan viewed these issues from a simple conservative perspective.

The significance of employing political ideology theory in the study of presidential leadership style and policy-making is that it is a good framework of analysis for examining Reagan's policy. Reagan's conservative political ideology manifested on his political agenda and strategy. This essay examines the origin of Reagan's political ideology and how it affects his political leadership style and political agenda. It also explains the meaning of the 1980 and 1984 elections as they relate to the Reagan administration's formulation of conservative public policy. The final section explains how he was able to influence the domestic policy-making process.

REAGAN'S POLITICAL IDEOLOGY: THE ORIGIN
OF REAGAN'S CONSERVATIVE VALUES

Reagan learned at an early age that energy and hard work were the essential qualities necessary for success as explained in Reagan's autobiography, *Where's the Rest of Me?*[1]

Reagan's early education was based on habits of hard work and industry, character building, pride in country and learning about the nation. Reagan attended small Eureka College in 1928. His early education reinforced his beliefs that the United States is the greatest country on earth and that the white race is the greatest race on earth. College for Reagan was a vehicle for personal advancement into the society.

Identifying with old-style American values was not only the product of Reagan's small-town beginnings and schooling, but also part of the era. During the 1920s, it was part of the allegiance to American values. The mood at this time was that of rugged honesty of the New England hills, rural virtues, clean living, religious faith, and public probity. Reagan, as president, tried to achieve these familiar verities. These were derived from the era of the 1920s.

Reagan explains in his book, Where's the Rest of Me?

> There is no left or right, or an up or down, up to the maximum of individual freedom consistent with law and order, or down to the ant heap of totalitarianism, and regardless of their humanitarian purpose, those who would sacrifice freedom for security have, whether they know it or not, chosen this downward path. Plutarch Warned, the real destroyer of the liberties of the people is he who spread among them bounties, donations and benefits. I honestly believe it's better to create jobs by restoring the economy than to provide handouts.[2]

According to an article in the Los Angeles Times, in March of 1982, Reagan held a meeting with African American clergymen and said to them, "Some well-meaning government program robbed recipients of their dignity, trapped them into a dependency that left them with idle time, less self-respect, and little prospect of a better future."[3] Reagan explained that his own life and personality were shaped by the traditional American values of his times that he wishes to bring back to the nation.

His rhetoric and ideas are characterized with such words as: self-help, hard work, autonomy, free enterprise, individualism, liberty, religion, morality and patriotism. Frank Van Der Linden wrote in a Reagan biography, "Certainly, he is old-fashioned. He clings to the traditions of courtesy, civility, and gentle manners. To the total disgust of sophisticates, he embodies all twelve traits of the Boy Scout Law: He is trustworthy, loyal, helpful, friendly, courteous, kind, obedient, cheerful, thrifty, brave, clean, and reverent".[4]

Obviously, Reagan's presidency was shaped by old-fashioned values about freedom, hard work, and morality. Also, the modern consumer culture was a big influence in shaping his ideas and activities in the White House. Despite Reagan's political rhetoric about the importance of traditional values, it was his career in entertainment and pleasure industries that had more impact on his life. His identity was shaped by a society where leisure and play were more important than work and where personal charm and conformity were more important to achieve success than personal initiative. Robert Dallek sums it up in his book as follows: "In his initial rise to stardom, Reagan was the consummate example not of the self-made man, but of the idol of consumption, with which millions of Americans could identify."[5]

His career in the entertainment industry followed a similar pattern of initiative coupled with lucky breaks on films. His success as a radio announcer at WHO in Des Moines encouraged him to become an actor. Reagan made a career in the entertainment industry by starring in a series of grade B movies. Due to his natural, down-home quality, most of his roles in the films seemed believable. According to Reagan, the combination of bluster, dumb chance, and some talent had opened the door to stardom.[6] He gained a permanent recognition as the Gipper when he played the role of George Gipp in the Knute Rockne Story.

The essence of George Gipp, whom Reagan portrayed in the film, was to play a part of an inspiring person who rose from obscurity to fame, which Reagan then used to further his cause. At the close of the movie, it reminded us of Gipp when the coach, Rockne, asked the Notre Dame football team to honor Gipp's death bed request by winning one for the Gipper. The significance of this movie to Reagan was that Knute Rockne's use of the story of Gipp's death to win the game and to inspire a team that was losing mainly because of division and low morale. The story gave the team the idea of what it is to play together, and to put aside their individual conflict for a common goal.

Reagan did not actually become a star until his performance in King's Row in 1941, which was the best film he made. He played a figure that loses both his legs after an accident. That role won Reagan acclaim and a new seven-year contract of one million dollars. In spite of his success in Hollywood, he was not comfortable. Robert Dallek concluded:

> His desire was to gain the sense of space and freedom, the feeling of independence and autonomy he has celebrated throughout his life. Indeed, Reagan's present-day prescription for the nation of a return to the old habits of self reliance, hard work, and moral constraint has a ring of personal urgency which makes one feel that he is pressing on the country what he would like to gain for himself".[7]

Yet, for all of Reagan's rhetoric of traditional American values, however powerful, his message was designed to reverse the modern trends, which he believed undermined freedom, and was turning people into semi automaton; he personified the consummate expression organization man, the other-directed personality who lacks genuine autonomy.

When Reagan was the governor of California, he seldom came up with any original idea, and often waited for a writer to feed him his lines and for a director to show him what to do like an actor. Reagan's celebration of the old-fashioned American value of work ethics and productivity is nothing but mere rhetoric. Reagan accumulated wealth and position mostly through the manipulation of personal charm rather than the old-fashioned way of hard labor. Despite his advocacy of hard work and productive labor, Reagan is a man of limited drive. Reagan was a detached and uninformed president during his years in office. Stating that there is a bitter White House power struggle that could badly affect his administration, Kondracke's article explained that Reagan was so far removed from the day-to-day workings of the White House that he was unaware of the dimension of the problem or possible consequences. The infighting was a disaster, an absolute disaster, out of control, with everybody having his own agenda. The president's aloofness often left him embarrassingly ignorant of the infighting. His top advisers often did not keep him fully informed of what was going on.[8]

A peculiar aspect of Reagan's personality was that a man who was the product of a consumer society was an advocate of rugged individualism and other traditional values. Reagan's beliefs were not of conscious hypocrisy but of genuine attachment to the small-town values of his early childhood. It is simplistic to deny that politics have been a projective arena for his personal feelings that are related only marginally to the external issues.

Reagan's early childhood implanted in him strong feelings about loss of control and self-possession, dependence and independence. He liked the idea of self-reliance, and his strong antipathy towards dependency. This was due partly, because of unrecognized fears that he may end up like his father. Indeed, what is interesting in the Reagan's life was his cherishing of freedom, autonomy, and self-mastery and his dislike for, or powerful feelings about the need to overcome, external control, and dependence on forces outside the individual. Reagan played out these roles in both his public and private lives.

REAGAN'S POLITICAL IDEOLOGY TRANSFORMATION

Ronald Reagan's political ideology was transformed from liberal to conservative in 1954, when he joined General Electric Corporation. Reagan's movie career suffered some setbacks from 1948 to 1954. Encouraged by his wife,

Nancy Reagan, he began to focus on national politics for autonomy and personal freedom from dependence. In 1954, Reagan accepted an offer from General Electric Corporation to be a host of a half-hour television show. Reagan became a promoter of the General Electric Corporation public image. His speeches were a morale booster for the company's employees whom he spent most of his time addressing. G.E. was a conservative corporation against big government and it was during this period that Reagan developed his views on big government.

Between 1954 and 1962, Reagan refined his political skills by speaking to live conservative audiences. He spoke to a large audience of G.E. employees whom he described as a cross-section of America who were interested in the truth and their personal liberties. During this period his speeches were focused on collectivism and the concentration of power in Washington, at the expense of loss of power to state and local governments. His speeches were for conservative audiences who believe that big government is dangerous to freedom. He wanted to remind them that the individual was, and should be forever, the master of his destiny. Reagan believed that freedom belonged to the individual by divine right. He attacked most of the social programs of big government,[9] calling the progressive income tax a Marxist tool for creating a socialist nation and declared that Social Security was an unfair restraint on those who could do better by themselves.

This ideology was a big transformation from Reagan's identification with Roosevelt and the liberal Democratic Party. Obviously, Reagan had become a rich conservative who did not like to pay high taxes, and he was a spokesperson for a conservative corporation who also resented government interfering with business. Without a doubt, this belief helped in converting Reagan into a conservative Republican.

Reagan's major reason for supporting Roosevelt's liberal policies in the New Deal era and condemning social programs and big government as a Republican can be found in his inner self and his penchant for saving others from dependency and defeat. He believed that Roosevelt was fighting for each person's freedom from want and dependency, and to restore the dignity of the individual. He made everyone feel that they counted. He believed that Roosevelt's message to the American people during the Great Depression was more of a call for renewed self-confidence and courage than an economic message.

Despite the fact that Ronald Reagan has fully changed from FDR liberalism to conservative Republican, he refused to accept the fact of his transformation. He argued that the Democrats had departed from the New Deal values and that he was still fighting for the same values of personal liberty and the dignity of the individual. Reagan believed that FDR was fighting for the forgotten man at the bottom of the economic pyramid and he, Reagan, was

fighting for the forgotten American, the man in the suburbs working to support his family and being over-taxed to help support someone else.

Reagan, as FDR Democrat, attacked big business leaders by calling them
greedy corporations, which inflated the economy and undermined the independence of their employees by making too much profit. Reagan as a conservative Republican attacked big government rather than big business. To
Reagan, the problem was the same, loss of individual freedom through collectivism and centralization of power. Reagan saw Roosevelt as an inspira-
tional figure. Such identification was what Reagan needed to launch his own
serious political career. William Leuchtenburg agreed:

> His self-identification with Roosevelt served him in several ways; it associated
> him with the last president historians have placed in the great category. It per-
> mitted him to leap over comparison to more recent predecessors such as Gold-
> water, which would have been awkward. It suggested that, like FDR, Reagan
> would inaugurate a new era, construct an enduring political coalition, contribute
> an imaginative domestic agenda, and originate a foreign policy that would re-
> shape the world. And it reassured those of the Democratic followers who con-
> tinued to have warm memories of the Roosevelt of their youth.[10]

Ronald Reagan's self-identification with Franklin Roosevelt was as much
emotional as political. Roosevelt's style, his ability to move people, his strong
image as an American hero, a great president who saved the nation during depression, all these mirrored Reagan's view of himself. Lou Cannon stated,
"Reagan's style has remained frankly and fervently Rooseveltian throughout
his life. His cadences are Roosevelt's cadences; his metaphors are the off-
spring of FDR's." Although Reagan does not support some of the New Deal
programs anymore, because of his devotion to personal self-control and individual freedom, Reagan still sees FDR as the successful hero that he himself
wanted to be. In the eyes of Reagan, Roosevelt was the father he never had,
the accomplished, courageous man who overcame a crippling disease to help
others become independent and to help the country regain its self-regard.

Although Reagan had a strong admiration for Roosevelt, by 1964 he had
become a prominent spokesman for the conservative Republicans. Reagan
became involved in Barry Goldwater's campaign. In 1964, he delivered a
speech supporting Goldwater's campaign, titled "A Time for Choosing" and
Reagan's political career was launched.

In the nationally televised address, Reagan strongly argued for Goldwater's
conservative cause. The theme of the speech was freedom, independence, and
self-control.

> So we have come to a time for choosing,......... either we accept the responsi-
> bility for our own destiny, or we abandon the American Revolution and confess

that an intellectual belief in a far-distant capital can plan our lives for us better than we can plan them ourselves. .... You and I have a rendezvous with destiny. We can preserve for our children this, the last best hope of man on earth or we can sentence them to take the first step into a thousand years of darkness.[11]

With this address, Reagan rose to a prominent conservative Republican. Reagan believed that he had found "the rest of me." Ronald Reagan's lifelong battle against inner fears of crippling dependence, his pursuit for autonomy that his father never had, all of these he transformed into a campaign to save America from forces that he believed were destroying the country.

REAGAN'S POLITICAL AGENDA

According to David Stockman, the architect of Reaganomics or trickle down economics, the Reagan Revolution declared a frontal assault on the welfare state. It demanded an immediate end to welfare for all able-bodied Americans. The administration had a tumultuous national referendum on everything in welfare program. The former Reagan's Budget Director stated that the failure of Reagan Revolution to trickle to the poor represents the triumph of politics over a particular doctrine of economic governance.[12] The Reagan revolution is based on an established conservative political ideology and a clear political agenda.

According to Nathan Glazer,[13] Reagan came to power with an agenda like no other president since Roosevelt. Various groups' interests were in jeopardy, the poor, African Americans, Hispanic Americans, the handicapped, college students, and even the environmental and consumer protection interests.

His proposed plan was based on his resentment of governmental intervention and high taxes, but rest on fairly coherent ideological themes. He attacked government inefficiency and the ineffectiveness. However, its underlying force was a vision of how America can grow economically and what makes us strong. He agued that individual activity, unhampered by government, stimulate economic growth. Special attention to the poor undermines the incentives to work. Government should not intervene so that individuals can take care of themselves, and can contribute to the economic growth of the country.

Reagan introduced supply-side economics, which was later called Reaganomics, as a sophisticated device for carrying out what he simply viewed as rational policy for the national economy. Reagan believed that tax cuts would give the individual and the corporation the initiative to invest; and that such investment would result in increased economic activities which would reduce inflation; the benefits would trickle down to the poor, eliminate racial discrimination, reduce the deficit, and provide the funds for increase in national defense programs.

Reagan's agenda called for a new direction, challenging Keynesian economic theory. The administration argued that the government would recognize its limitations in planning and managing the economic and social programs of a complex industrial society. Government should place more emphasis on the initiatives of the individual, private corporations, state and local governments. The administration's commitment to the federalism of the original United States' Constitution was based on the argument that the role of the federal government in economic and social programs should be limited.

Reagan's first inaugural speech was a powerful declaration of his agenda, a forceful expression that the ways and means to solve national economic problem was through less government. He argued:

> In this present crisis, government is not the solution to our problem; government is the problem. ....It's not my intention to do away with government. It is rather to make it work—work with us, not over us; to stand by our side, not to ride on our back. Government can and must provide opportunity, not smother it; foster productivity, not stifle it.........It is no coincidence that our present troubles paralleled and are proportionate to the intervention and intrusion in our lives that result from unnecessary and excessive growth of government.........It is time to reawaken this industrial giant, to get government back within its means and to lighten our punitive tax burden. And these will be our first priorities, and on these principles there will be no compromises.[14]

Reagan had no specific means for making his agenda work when he first won the governorship of California. As president of the United States, he had the supply-side economics also known as Reaganomics. Reaganomics was designed to reduce government spending on social programs, lowering taxes and balancing the budget. The theory assumed that tax breaks for the rich and private corporations will result into a major economic boom, which would create more jobs and generates more revenues to lower the federal deficit. The administration also increased funds for national defense build-up. George Bush called the agenda during the 1980 Republican Campaign "Voodoo economics," arguing that no such economic principle can reduce inflation and unemployment at the same time.

Richard Hofstadter argued that Reaganomics, advertised as an economic program, was more of symbolic politics, and ideology to rescue middle class and rich people from government tyranny and to eliminate immoral deficits and the government's special treatment of the poor, minority and special interest groups. It was a form of symbolic politics to assure that government would pay more attention to the demands of the white middle class and that the white male symbolically would once again be at the center of American politics.[15]

In a nationally televised address on the economy, on February 5, 1981, Reagan, the superb salesman, offered a plausible explanation on the problems facing the nation: "runaway deficits of almost $80 billion" for the 1980–81 fiscal year, the first consecutive years of double-digit inflation since World War I; mortgage interest rates that had gone up two and a half times higher than in 1960; a dollar is worth only thirty-six cents of its value in 1960; an inflated housing market in which only one out of eleven families could afford to buy their first home. This amounted to about 100 percent increase in twenty years of federal taxes taken from earnings, 7 million unemployed Americans and "the lowest rate of gain in productivity of virtually all the industrial nations with which we must compete in the world market."[16]

According to Reagan, the cause of the problems were uncontrollable government spending. The federal employees on payroll were 500 percent higher than in 1960. Federal government regulations added $100 billion a year to the cost of goods and services. The deficit was high because the government was borrowing and spending the money without restraint or control. Reagan administration believed that the solution to the economic problem was to increase productivity by making it possible for industry to modernize, and that means bringing government spending back within government revenues, which is the only way, and with increased productivity, inflation can be eliminated.

The administration's first step was to give instruction to government agencies not to fill any vacant positions. Reagan set up a task force committee under Vice-President Bush to eliminate many government regulations. Reagan also proposed tax cuts and a reduction in government spending to stimulate productivity and lower unemployment and inflation. He promised that the cut in government spending would not be "at the expense of the truly needy." Further cuts in social programs would affect only those "not really qualified." This proposal means hope to "restore the freedom of all men and women to excel and to create and to leave our children ....liberty in a land where every individual has the opportunity to be whatever God intended us to be."[17]

In an address on economic recovery, delivered to Congress on February 18, 1981, Reagan presented a comprehensive four-point agenda, consisting of cutting government spending and taxes, getting rid of unnecessary regulations and encouraging "a consistent monetary policy aimed at maintaining the value of the currency." Specifically, he asked Congress to reduce direct government spending by $41.4 billion by 1982. This would allow an increase of $40.9 billion above 1981 spending, which would assure a social safety net for the poverty-stricken, the disabled, and the elderly. Social Security and Medicare payments would not be cut. Reagan requested a 30 percent across-the-board tax cut over the next three years. His economic recovery program also included a tax cut on unearned income and an increase in depreciation allowances for corporations. Reagan promised to "come to grips with inefficient and burdensome regulations—eliminate those we can and reform the others." He directed the Federal Reserve System not to "allow money growth to increase consistently faster than the growth of goods and services."[18]

The Reagan political agenda appealed to millions of Americans, especially the white middle-class, who saw their interest included in the program. This agenda also provided an irresistible easy way out of the economic difficulties. Although most sophisticated Americans knew the agenda was too good to be true. Congress and the country went along with the agenda because it promised lower taxes, business expansion, and more jobs, less inflation, lower interest rates, smaller deficits, and greater military strength. After the president's speech in February on economic recovery, more than two-thirds of American people supported his economic program.

THE REAGAN ELECTIONS

1980 Election

There have been various interpretations of the significance of elections in a democratic government. Elections are legitimate processes, operating to give the elected leaders the authority to govern. This section is concerned with the Reagan elections as a democratic process by which a president is held accountable to the people. The concern is to understand how President Reagan's election gave the American voters a fair opportunity to render the president responsive to their wishes and to evaluate his performance in office. The dictates of the electoral process forced President Reagan to be accountable to certain political elites who were drawn from the ranks of those of high economic, educational, and occupational status. This bias is more ideological than socio-economic. The electoral process forced President Reagan to be more responsive to the elites who were more able to punish or reward him for his performance in office than the broad electorate. The electoral process put Reagan under pressure to be responsive to those with narrow interest and those of the right political wing.

Reagan won a decisive victory during the 1980 presidential election. He received 50.7 percent of the popular vote while Carter received 41 percent. Reagan won 489 of the Electoral College and 44 states and Carter won 44 of the Electoral College, carrying 6 states and the District of Columbia. In 1980, the Republicans gained 12 Senate seats, giving them a majority of 53 to 47, the largest margin in Senate since 1928. In the house, Republicans gained 33 seats and reduced the Democratic seats by about 40 percent, from 276 to 243 for Democrats, and Republicans seats increased from 159 to 192. With Reagan winning the presidency and Republicans gaining seats in the Senate and House, the 1980 election represented a significant shift to the right.[19]

Reagan's victory was a result of only a few eligible voters voting in the 1980 election. Only about 55.1 percent of the voters went to the polls in 1980, and Reagan won 28 percent of the eligible votes. His victory can be viewed as continuation of voters' alienation and nonparticipation that started in the 1960s.[20] The voters' turnout was the lowest in a national election since 1948. The 1980 Reagan election clearly showed that the American voters were dissatisfied with the government, the economy and President Jimmy Carter. In short, Reagan's victory may be more of dissatisfaction with the Carter administration than a turn to the right or attraction to Reagan.

Reagan viewed his victory as a mandate for massive changes in the domestic policy. Reagan believed that the mandate provided him with the authority to carry out his conservative political agenda. Interpretation of this mandate means radical dismantling of the liberal social welfare state. John L. Palmer and Isabel Sawhill stated, "Perhaps the single most important advantage that the Reagan administration enjoyed going into its first year was the widespread impression that it had won a substantial mandate from the voters for a bold departure in national policy."[21]

Several arguments in contrast to the so-called election mandate, however, agreed that the Reagan election of 1980 was not a mandate from the American people for a radical change in domestic policy. The general public was asked whether the 1980 vote was more of a rejection of Carter or a mandate to Reagan and his conservative political agenda. Sixty-three percent of those polled said Reagan's victory was mostly a rejection of the Carter administration, whereas only 24 percent felt it was a mandate for conservatism. Even Republicans (54 to 34 percent) and some conservatives (57 to 30 percent) said that the election was more of a rejection of Carter administration's policies than a conservative mandate.

Although voters supported Reagan's platform slightly more than they supported Carter's stand, the 1980 election was largely interpreted as a decisive mandate by the Reagan administration. The main reason given was that the electoral vote margin was one of the highest since 1932. In addition, the congressional seats gained by the Republicans helped strengthen the impression that Reagan's election was a strong mandate from the American people. However, voters did not support the specifics of the Reagan agenda, they were asking for a new direction. Even though the public poll showed that the 1980 election signified a strong call for moderate change, Reagan's administration saw it as a strong mandate for radical change in public policy, Congress, the press, and the public were ready to go along with the new direction.

1984 Election

Reagan's reelection in 1984 represented changes in the fundamental elements of American electoral politics. The election of 1984 brought a major realignment to American politics, probably the most significant since the end of World War II. Such a fundamental realignment of American politics was occurring along ideological fault lines. Party identification was on the rise but the Democratic lead over Republican loyalties was declining from 17 points in 1976 to 10 points in 1984, the lowest margin in three decades.[22] Warren E. Miller explained, "The aftermath of the successes of the civil rights movement two decades earlier produced a partial realignment with the solidification of black allegiances to the Democratic Party and an offsetting movement of whites, disproportionately southern whites, into Republican ranks."[23]

However, the realignment that resulted from the struggles of the 1960s and 1970s did reestablish many of the components of the traditional Democratic coalition in national politics. The social-economic structures that are made up of various ethnic groups and urban poor, who allied against the traditional counterpart centers of Republican support, maintained their support for the Democratic Party up to the election of Reagan in 1980 and partially into the Democratic resurgence in 1982. The election of 1984 brought a new theme stressing the ideological differences between the Democratic Party and the Republican Party. The election of 1984 signifies the beginnings of a change in partisan loyalties.

The realignment that took place in the 1984 election was greater than any since the election of 1964. Of more importance, however, and with greater implications for the future of fundamental American electoral politics, were the qualitative nature and structural locations of the surge in Republican loyalties and the decrease in Democratic loyalties. The ideological party realignment was more significant than party identification in determining the result of the election of 1984.

The 1984 election can be interpreted on the basis of changes that took place between the two elections of 1980 and 1984. During this period the national economy was experiencing drastic change in budget and tax cuts, the issues of double-digit unemployment and inflation were replaced by the rhetoric of economic stability and forecasts of new economic growth and prosperity. Even though there was a high interest rate and a high unemployment rate in 1982, by 1984 the election theme was new economic growth and prosperity. Reagan's 1984 campaign was free of any burden, unlike Carter's 1980 campaign and the Iranian hostage crisis. Both domestic and international news continued to be good news. However, global and domestic crises that had contributed in the defeat of incumbent presidents in the past since 1968 disappeared and gave Reagan the advantage to enter reelection campaign and win the 1984 election.

No one knew for sure if the positive turn of events was as a result of the Reagan administration's policies. However, it was obvious to critics and admirers alike that the administration had formulated social policy that was designed to change the role of government. The image of the administration's goals gave new meaning to the established and largely unchanging policy preferences of majority of the electorate. This change, in reality as well as in perception, is partly responsible in accounting for the voters' decisions at the ballot box in the election of 1984. It was seen as a sign of the electorate's appreciation of Regan's economic policy and a nation at peace. Therefore, the outcome of the voters' evaluation of the president's performance was clearly different from that of 1980.

The negative perception that resulted from Carter being perceived as a failed president led to a popular call to move away from liberal policies. That call was answered by Reagan administration with a drastic turn to the right. The 1980 election outcome signified more of the rejection of a failed president and not an opposition to his administration's policies, nor a clear mandate to Reagan. The rhetoric that there was a mandate calling for big reduction in governmental activity may have been over emphasized.

Indeed, there was no increase in public sentiment supporting the Reagan's position on a variety of questions of public policy, support that would show the electorate's responding to the new change in governmental roles. Furthermore, despite the fact that there was a conservative administration in the White House, there was no apparent increase of popular support for the administration on its conservative ideology.

REAGAN'S POLITITRATEGY FOR
CONTROLLING DOMESTIC POLICY PROCESS

Reagan the "Great Communicator" used his presidential power very effectively to persuade Congress to legislate, regulators to regulate, and bureaucrats to carry out his agenda. His principal responsibility was to move the machinery of the political process into action. William Ker Muir captured the essence of Reagan's power in the following statement:

> Ronald Reagan exercised a great deal of presidential power in his eight years in the White House. Admittedly, he was far from perfectly effective. Still, he did obtain the favorable action of Congress on all his major initiatives: control of runaway inflation, tax rate reductions, the termination of new federal domestic welfare spending, legislation requiring a balanced federal budget and providing a tolerable transition to this end, tax reform on a comprehensive scale, reduction

of federal regulations in the private sector, and strengthened the assessment of his most severe critics, Ronald Reagan stirred up a lot of governmental action.[24]

The challenge facing many presidents has always been to make sure that several policies formulated within the administration meet the political ideology and agenda of the regime, Ronald Reagan met the challenge with a strong political strategy. Focusing on using the White House staff to influence or directly control the policy direction to suit his programmatic and political goals, Reagan's major strategy was persuasion not coercion. "Reagan was strategy smart," argued Aaron Wildavsky. "The more a politician alters prevailing policies and expectations concerning behavior while moving events in the desired direction, that movement and direction being compatible with democratic norms, the better the strategist."[25] Shirley Anne Warshaw commented:

> Reagan built on the experience of his predecessors and continued the use of a White House structure for managing domestic policy-making. The legacy of the Reagan years, however, is that the administration expanded the White House structure to include not only the domestic policy office, but also a network of interrelated White House offices to oversee departmental policy-making. The White House exercised more control over domestic policy under Reagan than in any previous administration.[26]

Reagan's structure for influencing domestic policymaking involved three basic units in the White House: The Office of Policy Development which was responsible for guiding departmental initiatives; the White House Office of Personnel which was responsible for departmental political appointees, ensuring that those appointees were Reagan loyalists; and a White House internal clearance system, which allowed White House staff to bargain the administration's policies with Congress. Such a multi-structural approach was designed to get the entire senior White House staff involved.

As soon as Reagan administration assumed office, it changed the Carter administration's Domestic Policy Group to the Office of Policy Development. It served notice that a new administration had taken over and would put its own okay on all domestic affairs. The Office of Policy Development (OPD) was created by the administration to manage Reagan's domestic policy initiatives. The OPD designed an organizational relationship between the White House and various departments to make sure those programs were designed, based on the Reagan political ideology and agenda. This was a structure that enabled the White House to have constant interaction with senior staff members of each department. Programs developed by the departments were in line with the Office of Policy Development, which detailed the administration's positions on all public policy. All cabinet members were provided with detailed information called notebooks. These notebooks detailed Reagan's ideology and agenda from the 1980 campaign on a wide variety of policy issues. Each department officer was instructed to base all of their program development on the presidential goals and objectives detailed in the notebooks.

Reagan was deeply committed to controlling the cabinet to suit his philosophy. The administration designed a policy structure in which the heads of every agency and department were fully involved with the White House. Reagan carefully screened his appointees based on ideological consistency. He selected executives who were loyal in their commitment to his ideology and policy. For a better control of the cabinet, the department and agency heads were organized into a cabinet council system made up of five to six councils. The president was the chairman of each council; the cabinet secretary chaired the council in the absence of the president. The cabinet members, the vice-president, and members of the senior White House staff attended each of the cabinet meetings. Sometimes, the chairman of CEA and the director of OMB also attended council meetings. Meetings were held frequently and President Reagan presided in twenty-six of those council meetings during his two terms in office.[27]

Another one of Reagan's strategies for controlling the public policy process was personnel selection and management. As we have seen, Reagan had a significant amount of control over the department policy development through the cabinet council member meetings. The administration also controlled the subcabinet personnel involved in department policy development. Cabinet members were chosen for their ideological commitment to the Reagan goals and objectives. Lower level cabinet officers were also selected for their ideological beliefs. All political appointments were scrutinized and selections were made, based on their commitment to the Reagan political ideology and agenda.

Reagan presidentialized the bureaucracy. There was a fear by the White House that the career bureaucrats would try to oppose Reagan policies. The administration then moved to replace top management officers with Reagan loyalists and stop the promotion of career bureaucrats. The administration sought to add more layers of political appointees on top of career bureaucrats. The Heritage Foundation, a conservative research institution, presented Reagan administration prior to inauguration with an action paper warning them of how powerful the bureaucracy was:

> Career bureaucratic subordinates engaging in covert inter-bureaucratic struggle to block his initiatives should not surprise the political executive who is promoting significant policy change within his department. Bureaucratic opponents will lobby vigorously against the proposed policy change to client groups, congressional committee staffs, and the press. The bureaucracy's resources for defending

its viewpoint, leaking discrediting material, and mustering outside allies are such
that it could be correctly called the "ultimate lobby."[28]

The personnel were made up of loyalists to the Reagan agenda with top
management experience. Unlike Carter who was interested in technical ex-
perts for cabinet, subcabinet and managerial posts, Reagan was interested in
people with ideological commitment to his agenda. Some cabinet members
tried to oppose the amount of control that the administration had over personnel selection, but were eventually forced to conform. Reagan's Personnel
Office was part of the White House gateway, closing the doors on those who
do not agree with Reagan's ideology. The duty was doing the president's bidding to help him be chief executive and in fact in full control.

A third strategy of the Reagan administration's control of the public
policy-making process involved the legislative strategy group. Reagan controlled the departmental development of domestic policies to ensure their
compliance with the White House political agenda. The White House had to
plan a strategy to win congressional approval. The legislative strategy group
was made up of OMB director David Stockman, Treasury Secretary Donald
Regan, White House Councilor Edwin Meese and Chief of Staff James Baker.
The role of the strategy group was to develop effective public relations and
legislative strategy for the president's policy. The legislative strategy group
provided another layer of White House control of the domestic policy formulation process and thereby reduced the power of the agencies and departments
in policy development. Warshaw said "Baker regularly dealt with Congress
on policy issues without any input from the departments."[29]

Usually, the congressional liaison in any president's administration con-
sulted with the agencies and departments to modify any program that may not
pass through Congress. This process traditionally takes time; the Reagan's administration's strategy was to modify the proposal without working with the
departments and through the cabinet council system. James Baker, heading
the legislative strategy group, developed this most advantageous system of
securing congressional support for Reagan's domestic policy without going
through the normal process.

President Reagan's strategy to control the policy process was effective in
passing legislation. Presidents can maximize their political assets by presenting the most important proposals early in their administration; keep the legislation simple, and concentrating on mobilizing support for it. Reagan did exactly that. It had a clear, simple political agenda, and acted immediately to
win support. In the early weeks of Reagan's regime, he quickly presented his
fiscal policy to Congress.

Reagan did not wait for the beginning of the fiscal cycle to present his fiscal package to Congress. He therefore avoided the unnecessary political

struggle that beset other presidents. His concentration on the budget package enabled him to control the process before his opponents started organizing political opposition. Congress sympathizing with the president's agenda, having no clear alternatives to offer, and fearing that opposition would lead to political suicide, Congress was predisposed to follow Reagan's lead.

Reagan centralized the policy-making process more than any other president in modern history. The White House became the center of policy development, management, and implementation. Personnel within the departments were cleared through the White House. The White House and the Executive Office of the President constantly monitored the actions of Bureaucrats. The legacy of the Reagan is that it created a system of control that his predecessors started, but did not fully developed. Reagan's administration designed a system of controlling domestic policy from the White House that was based on conservative political ideology.

NOTES

1. Ronald Reagan and Richard G. Hubler, *Where's the Rest of Me?* (New York: Duell, Sloan and Pearce, 1965).

2. Reagan, *Where's the Rest of Me?* , 303.

3. Los Angeles Times, (27 March 1982): 9.

4. Frank Van Der Linden. *The Real Reagan* (New York: William Morrow, 1981), 25–26.

5. Robert Dallek, *Ronald Reagan: The Politics of Symbolism* (Cambridge, Mass.: Harvard University Press, 1984) 9.

6. Ronald Reagan, *Where's the Rest of Me?* 69.

7. Robert Dallek, Ronald Reagan, 12.

8. Morton Kondracke, "Reagan's I. Q.," *The New Republic* (24 March 1982), 9–12.

9. Bill Boyarsky, *The Rise of Ronal Reagan* (New York: Random House, 1968): 101.

10. William Leuchtenburg, "Ronald Reagan's Liberal Past," *The New Republic* (23 May 1983), 18–25.

11. Kurt Ritter and David Henry, Ronald Reagan: *The Great Communicator* (New York: Greenwood, 1992), 135–143.

12. David Stockman, *The Triumph of Politics: How the Reagan Revolution Failed* (New York: Harper & Row, 1986), 8.

13. Nathan Glazer, "The Social Policy of the Reagan Administration," in *The Social Contract Revisited*, ed. Lee Bawden (Washington, D.C.: Urban Institute, 1984), 223.

14. Ronald Reagan, "Inaugural Address, January 20, 1981," *Public Papers of the Presidents* (Washington, D.C.: 1981), 1.

15. Richard Hofstadter, *The Paranoid Style in American Politics* (New York: Alfred A. Knopf, 1981), 81–87.

16. Ronald Reagan, "Address to the Nation on the Economy, February 5, 1981," *Public Papers of the Presidents* (Washington, D.C.: 1981), 79.

17. Ronald Reagan, "Address to the Nation on Economy, February 5, 1981," 66.

18. Ronald Reagan, "Economic Recovery Address, February 18, 1981," *Public Papers of the Presidents*, 108.

19. Robert Dallek, Ronald Reagan, 60.

20. John L. Palmer and Isabel Sawhill, eds., *The Reagan Experiment: An Examination of Economic and Social Policies under Reagan Administration* (Washington, D.C.: Urban Institute, 1982), 142–144.

21. Lester M. Salomon and Alan J. Abramson, "Governance," in *The Reagan Record: The Assessment of America's Changing Domestic Priorities*, ed. John L. Palmer and Isabel Sawhill (Washington, D.C.: Urban Institute, 1984), 37.

22. Lester M. Salomon, "Governance," 293.

23. Warren E. Miller, "The Election of 1984 and the Future of American Politics," in *Elections in America*, ed. Kay L. Schlozman (Boston: Allen & Unwin, 1987), 304.

24. William Ker Muir, *The Bully Pulpit: The Presidential Leadership of Ronald Reagan* (San Francisco: Institute for Contemporary Studies, 1992), 189.

25. Aaron Wildavsky, "President Reagan as a Political Strategist," in *Election in America*, ed. Kay L. Schlozman (Boston: Allen & Unwin, 1987), 221.

26. Shirley Anne Warshaw, "White House Control of Domestic Policy Making: The Reagan Years," *Public Administration Review* (May–June 1995), 248.

27. Margaret Jane Wyszomirski, "The Role of a Presidential Office for Domestic Policy: Three Models and Four Case," in *The Presidency and Public Policy Making* ed. George Edwards, et al. (Pittsburgh: University of Pittsburgh, 1985), 141.

28. Stuart Butler et al., *Mandate for Leadership II* (Washington, D.C.: Heritage Foundation, 1984), 491.

29. Shirley Anne Warshaw, "White House Control of Domestic Policy Making, 251."

Chapter Three

Unemployment Theory and Government Policy

The controversy about unemployment has gained a great deal of attention in recent years, and considering the current rate of unemployment among certain groups, the prediction is that unemployment will continue to be a volatile issue in American politics for a long time. For a clear understanding of public policy and unemployment, this chapter will begin by defining the nature and cause of unemployment, followed by an explanation of how unemployment policy changes over time, and concludes with a discussion of the attempts made in the past by presidents and lawmakers to respond to the unemployment problems. The explanation in this section will provide us with important political terms for understanding the facts about unemployment problems and how to evaluate the public policy impact.

Unemployment is a public policy issue of the highest rank. It commands the attention of national political figures, various interest groups, the media, scholars and the American public. One of the single most visible signs of the national economic growth is the unemployment rate, which is the percentage of people unable to find work when they want jobs. The costs of unemployment are tremendous; a one percent increase in the unemployment rate will decrease the federal treasury tax revenues by about $30 billion and spending in such programs as unemployment insurance, welfare payment and food stamps will increase.

The costs of unemployment also can be measured in social and personal terms. Unemployment can result in crime, alcohol and drug abuse, spousal as well as child abuse, family disintegration, physical and mental illness. The unemployed often lose their health, property, and hope for the future. The victims of unemployment loose more than just jobs, their plights are endless. Stephen K. Bailey explained:

> In the broadest perspective of time, the modern concern about full employment is but the latest version of man's age-old petition "Give us this day our daily bread." If attention is now addressed to Washington rather than to heaven, it is only because man has changed his mind about the relative competence of God and government in dealing with pressing economic issues.[1]

Although elected officials and government at all levels are trying to do something about the problems of unemployment, there are still deep divisions on what and how the government should approach and solve unemployment. The decision on how policymakers should handle the problem is a difficult task. The solutions proposed by many presidents, lawmakers, and scholars reflect various definitions of the unemployment controversy. The proposals are reflections of political ideologies and opinions about public and private strategies, and about what the government should do to achieve the policy objectives. Formulating a comprehensive public policy to alleviate unemployment problems involves a difficult political process.

A fundamental American political issue for over 50 years is how the United States government should help the unemployed. In the 1980s, unemployment problems probably gained more attention than at any time since the Great Depression. For the first time since 1937 the public, in 1982, ranked unemployment as the single most important problem facing the nation. During the 1970s, the high cost of living or inflation was ranked higher than unemployment. In the 1960s the issue of war and peace was considered most important.[2] Presidents, lawmakers, party leaders, labor leaders, and policy analysts provided possible solutions designed to guarantee economic growth and full employment. As the controversy grew, the national goals of full employment for all Americans seemed impossible to reach.

One of the goals of the American economic and political agenda is that of providing full employment. It has been achieved more in wartime than in peacetime and more for some groups than for others. During the 1980s, the unemployment rate in the United States was 7.4 percent; among blacks it was 14.8 percent; 18.8 percent among teenagers; 9.7 percent among women and 10.5 percent among Hispanics.[3] These statistics present a direct affront to American goals and aspirations. It also demonstrates the need for special policies on behalf of the groups with high levels of unemployment.

What is full employment? The answer to this question is not readily apparent. Full employment can mean different things to different people. William Beveridge defined full employment as "having always more vacant jobs than unemployed men, not slightly fewer jobs."[4] There are ways unemployment in the United States can be reduced to a level lower than it is. A variety of proposals contradict the fatalistic belief that the United States cannot do more than it is doing to create more jobs and reduce unemployment. Certainly, a combination of structural public policies and demand stimulation can be employed to achieve the 4 percent unemployment level, generally accepted as the full employment rate.

CAUSES OF HIGH UNEMPLOYMENT RATE

In analyzing the distinct pattern of the unemployment rates, three categories can be identified. They are frictional, cyclical, and structural unemployment. Frictional unemployment occurs as a result of the normal labor turnover that arises in a viable dynamic economy. Sometimes employees change jobs, lose jobs, or leave the labor force. At any given time, employees may find jobs or may decide to stop looking for work, while others may enter or re-enter the labor force. Even in the best of healthy economies, there is some unemployment that arises from these dynamic frictions in the economy.

Cyclical unemployment is the type that is perhaps perceived and felt most severely. Cyclical unemployment is associated with business cycles. Decreases in aggregate demand that occurs during recessions also cause a decline in the demand for labor. The real wage rate does not respond to the change, which means that the real wage rate does not decline as the demand for labor declines. Cyclical unemployment occurs due to this change in business cycles. Cyclical unemployment is temporary. Even a permanent decline in aggregate demand results in only temporary unemployment because, after a while, wages will adjust to equate labor supply and demand in a competitive economy.

The least understood and the most traumatic type to endure is structural unemployment. Unlike cyclical unemployment, structural occurs due to shifts in the relative demand for different types of labor. Changes in relative factor prices like oil prices, changes in technology, changes in institutions, changes in tastes and performance, or changes in other characteristics of the economy can cause these relative shifts in labor demand. Thus, as demand for one type of labor declines, relative to another, a temporary shift occurs between the skills that employers are looking for and the skills available in the labor market.

This type of shift produces only temporary unemployment because, after a while, those who are structurally unemployed will either retrain to find employment in the now higher labor demand industries, relocate to find jobs in their field of specialty, or probably leave the labor force altogether. In the latter case they will not be counted as unemployed. No one knows exactly how many displaced workers are in the United States.

This type of unemployment poses difficult problems for public policy. Unlike the disadvantaged groups, the displaced workers often have stable job records in a single industry or trade and relatively few episodes of unemployment. At one time, their skill and education were enough to earn above average wages in their jobs. Now they find themselves without jobs in a labor market that has changed drastically since they joined the labor force years ago

The American automobile industry is a good example of industrial decline leading to worker displacement. The United States auto industry lost a great deal to the foreign/domestic automobile market. The shift in the auto industry can be attributed to the automakers' failure to produce fuel-efficient automobiles that would compete with foreign models, the high cost of labor in the United States, and the overall high cost of producing quality American automobiles. Also, the automation of the auto manufacturing industry eliminated many jobs. The change in the auto industry is just one example of shifts in the economy that displace permanent workers, causing them to join the labor force of the unemployed.

Unlike the cyclically unemployed, the structurally unemployed experience long periods of unemployment. Many people among the disadvantaged groups fall into the structural category. The disadvantaged are those people with little or no work experience, job training or education. Some of the disadvantaged depend on public assistance, some are 21 years of age or younger, many are from the minority groups, and others cannot speak or write English very well. In addition to lacking the skills and education required in the labor market, many disadvantaged people also experience racial, age, gender and ethnic discrimination

A significant percentage of these people were unemployed or discouraged from looking for work, others were the working poor, employed but earning income that was below the minimum level for poverty. The disadvantaged workers include high school dropouts, youths, minorities, women and the poor in general that lack the skills and education to gain meaningful employment in the American labor market. These groups of disadvantaged Americans remain unemployed, and on public assistance or are employed in menial jobs due to the lack of basic skills, education and discrimination. Without a comprehensive public policy, the future for these disadvantaged groups is bleak.

During Reagan regime, unemployment reached its highest level in the 1980s since Great Depression. In 1982, 10.8 percent of the labor force was unemployed, that is, more than one in five people were unemployed at sometime during the year, and more than 4 million Americans could not find jobs during the entire year. During the peak year of 1982, twelve million people could not find employment and another two million Americans were not counted among the category of the unemployed because they had given up looking for work. Among minority groups, the unemployment rate had nearly doubled the national average, and more than half of the youths could not find employment.[5]

The only other time in the post-World War II history of the United States that unemployment rose above 7 percent was during the 1973–1975 recession. This upsurge in the unemployment rate during the 1980s was the worst downturn in the United States economy since the Great Depression. American economy's worst experience with unemployment was during the Great Depression when one quarter of the labor force was unemployed and the unemployment rate stayed in the high teens for over ten years. The average unemployment rate for the 1950s and 1960s was 4.6 percent; the average unemployment rate for the 1970s climbed to 6.2 percent and the average for the 1980s was 9 percent, the highest since World War II. The United States annual unemployment rate has remained above 4 percent since the 1970s; 4 percent is the accepted level for a successful full employment public policy.[6]

The unemployment rate is the percent of work force that is unemployed. The short- and long-term shifts in the number in the work force affect the rate of unemployment. Workers must be employed or actively seeking jobs to be counted as a part of the labor force. There has been a steady increase in the labor force since the 1950s. There are more Americans and more of them are participating in the job market now than ever before. This increase in the size of the labor force reflects a significant change in the demographic and social shifts in the United States' society. The baby boomers that joined the labor market in the 1960s, 1970s, and 1980s brought an important demographic change in the labor force.

The increasing labor force is posing a great challenge to the economy and to policymakers to create more new jobs. In order to reduce the unemployment rate to one percent, the economy needs a real economic growth of 3 to 4 percent growth in excess of inflation. The real economic growth can be determined by the size and productivity of the work force.

Average hourly earning, advanced only 6.9 percent, leading to a 0.6 percent reduction in real earnings, annually. The cumulative wage lagged nearly 7 percent during the 1980s. Average hourly earnings also lagged behind the combined increase in prices and productivity by 1.4 percent annually and 16.7 percent cumulatively, resulting in a drastic drop in the available goods and services. This wage lag was one of the main reasons for the stagnation in the living standards of many Americans during the 1980s.

The 1980s recorded a tremendous increase in the number of high school and college graduates who joined the labor market. Hence, about 1 out of 4 Americans in the labor force, ages 25 to 64 had completed 4 or more years of college. Also, the rate with 1 to 3 years of college doubled to about 20 percent, whereas the rate of high school graduates increased from 35 to 40 percent. As a result, workers without high school diplomas dropped from 41 percent to 26 percent.[7]

Despite the increase in the educated labor force, the unemployment rate for 25 to 64 year olds increased to about 6 percent. Because the economy was going through an expansionary phase, the explanation of changes in aggregate unemployment between the 1970s and 1980s must focus on structural unemployment. Structural unemployment results from a fundamental mismatch between supply and demand of labor skills or vocational mismatches in the labor market.[8]

Education

Education has always reduced the probability of being unemployed. Education is a significant criterion for job market success over time. Although, the labor supply for both high school and college graduates has increased, there is a greater demand for college graduates than for high school graduates. Because of the enormous availability of both high school and college graduates, employers are more likely to employ workers with college degrees largely at the expense of demand for high school graduates, even in jobs that do not need complex or higher education. Often, in a growing economy, skills possessed by high school graduates do not match the skills desired for the new jobs that are available. This is the main reason why many older workers with less than a college education are being laid off from some industries that are going through changes. There is a mismatch between the jobs available and the skills of high school graduates who are entering the job market. High school graduates accounted for 60 percent of the unemployment rate in the 1980s while college graduates accounted for 8 percent.[9]

The competitive advantage held by college graduates will continue into the future, especially during the business cycle downturns, when the unemployment gap between high school and college graduates typically increases. The projection is that the size of college graduates who are reentering the labor force would continue to increase through the years. While few college graduates are likely to face long-term unemployment, the increase in the college graduate labor supply is affecting the jobs available for high school graduates. Apparently, the labor market problem will continue for most Americans without any college education because of employers' requirements for more educated and highly-skilled workers. The labor market is been crowded by the baby boom generation, and it has had a great impact on the unemployment rate, particularly, among the older unskilled workers and the high school dropouts.

Unemployment is caused by many complex and interdependent factors of the domestic and global economy. The rate of unemployment is determined by upswings and slowdowns in economic activity, expansion and decline in selected industries, long-term changes in the size and composition of the work force, technological innovations, energy prices, international trade, and shifting demands and supply for labor and special skills. However, public policy can have a direct or indirect impact on all of these factors. Though, it can be difficult to differentiate causes and effects, it is possible to examine significant trends that contribute to the nature and extent of the unemployment.

To explain the causes of high unemployment, we have to examine some factors that cause the unemployment rate to rise consistent with a given condition of the economy. The increase in the work force of youths and women, groups that have high rates of unemployment, social service programs and labor legislation that are believed to encourage benefit recipients not to work, the friction between wage and price-setting behavior. These are some of factors that affect the level of unemployment.

In fact, as we have seen, these factors, labor force, education, demographics, social and labor programs, and wage and price-setting behaviors influence the high level of unemployment. During the past few decades, each of these factors has received some form of attention by policy-makers and scholars. They have also been drastically reversed or reduced in the past. Although these factors are known to contribute to the high rate of unemployment, they should not pose any threat to achieving the full employment policy of 4 percent attained in the 1960s.

The state of the national economy is the fundamental determinant of the level of unemployment. Therefore, public policy to stimulate economic growth and demand for labor must be the central focus of any administration program to attain full employment at the 4 percent level. However, the make-up of the work force does not explain the total picture of unemployment because structural unemployment presents a very serious difficulty in determining the accurate composition of the labor force. The official unemployment rate does not estimate the true extent of the labor force problems because it excludes two types of workers, discouraged workers and part-time workers. Discouraged workers are those who have given up their search for jobs even though they want to work. Part-time workers are those who work part-time but would rather work full-time but could not find a full-time job.

During the first few years of Reagan administration, a survey by the Department of Labor estimated the number of discouraged workers to be about 1.6 million in 1983 and part-time workers to be about 6 million people.[10] The exclusion of these categories of workers in the calculation reduces the unemployment rate to a significantly lower official level. Public policy initiative is the key to solving these structural problems and reducing the unemployment rate to full employment level.

THEORIES OF UNEMPLOYMENT

There is a constant debate among scholars on the advantage of market force and the disadvantages of the market mechanism. Since Adam Smith, scholars have admired the efficiency, anonymity, and subtlety of a decentralized competitive market as a perfect mechanism for allocating resources and distributing income.[11] Proponents of the market mechanism stressed the advantage of free trade and flexible exchange rates favoring cash transfers over goods transfers; and they stress the disadvantages of such things as rent controls, interest rate ceilings, and minimum wage laws. Their opinion on free market policy issues does not represent conservative ideology because most scholars agree that equitable redistribution of income, especially to the poor and the disadvantaged, requires an effective government policy.

Simultaneously, scholars who oppose the free market mechanism because of its imperfections, point out the flaws in the price system and how market instruments fail to recognize the problems of an ideal society. The tension between market efficiency and market failure is more obvious in the demand and supply of the labor force. The labor market can relate immediately to a lot of things in the economy and the performance of the labor market is the most visible sign of the performance of the economy. Moreover, the labor market's special pathology, unemployment, is visible, unsettling and frustrating. The tension has led from theory to public policy and always generated controversial debate throughout the history of unemployment.

Classical Theory

Alfred Marshall, Jean Baptiste Say, and other classicists and neoclassicists, beginning with the eighteenth century, expressed their views on unemployment. Classical and neoclassical theories of unemployment focus on the transitory nature of unemployment; these theorists do not accept the premise that unemployment is involuntary except in the case of transitory phenomena that can be solved by lower wages. The central focus of the theory is that capitalism can regulate itself and its defenders advocate laissez-faire in the case of unemployment. Even during periods of high unemployment, the theory argues that government should do nothing to reduce high unemployment, but to keep its hands off the economy. The classicists prescribed orthodox economic measures of belt-tightening, lower wages and reducing government economic expenditures.

Marxian Theory

Marxian theory, which originated with socialist theorist Karl Marx in the nineteenth century, presents another view of unemployment. Karl Marx argued that unemployment is inevitable under capitalism. He explained that because of the alternating periods of expansion and contraction of the economy, the business cycle is the true means of capitalist development. Marx considered the unemployment as constituting an economic reserve army of surplus labor vital to the normal operation of a capitalist economy. As a readily available supply of labor, the unemployed permit the system to expand during the boom period. This industrial reserve grows large during periods of economic contraction when fewer laborers are needed or as a result of new technological innovations displacing labor. For capitalists to increase profit they introduced technology. In periods of high unemployment, wages are held down and that helps to increase profit. The pools of the unemployed can always replace employed workers. Another feature of capitalism is class struggle between the capitalists and the workers. According to Marx, this struggle is intensified by unemployment, which he believes will eventually contribute to the collapse of the capitalist economy. The Marxian theory strongly assents that capitalism without unemployment is as impossible as socialism with unemployment.

Most Marxian philosophers in the United States have little or no influence on most mainstream economists or on the policymakers because their theory has been pushed into the underworld of unemployment policy. Before the Great Depression of the 1930s, the classical and neoclassical views were predominant in their influence on public policy. The Great Depression destroyed the commanding authority that the classicists and neoclassicists had over Marxism. During the Depression, millions of lives were lost. People were looking for alternative theories. The stock market collapsed. The economy was in deep trouble; poverty, mass unemployment, class struggles, and chaos were in the society.

Keynesian Theory

The 1930s experienced a worldwide depression, and in 1936 John Maynard Keynes came out with a theory that filled a policy void. Keynes' view provided a strong intellectual base for government intervention in economic activities. Later, Keynes new unemployment theory received a great deal of attention among scholars and policymakers in America

Keynes agreed with Marx on the inevitability of the advanced capitalists system to create high levels of unemployment. In fact, Keynes saw unemployment as the major problem of the capitalist economy. He stressed that recurrent low demands for labor in the private sector contributed to the high unemployment not just high wages. He suggested that in order to avoid high unemployment, the government must actively intervene and increase expenditures during the sagging economy. Indeed, to Keynes, a capitalist economy could achieve full employment if adequate government expenditure and effective policy are designed to stimulate economic growth and demand for labor. Keynesian theory challenged the classical and neoclassical theories that government intervention is necessary to stimulate demand to achieve full employment. He also challenged the orthodox Marxist theory about the inevitability of unemployment in a capitalist system.

Contemporary unemployment theory, though obviously full of analytical innovation, has revived much of the old theoretical framework in slightly different forms. Modern theoretical innovations are interesting, but the basic controversial issues remain the same as the old questions. The most important issue facing the unemployment theory is the old tension between market efficiency and market failure.

Is the market efficient enough to solve the unemployment problem or is there imperfection in the labor market in addressing this issue of unemployment? Obviously, there is an imperfection in the ability of the labor market to clear at equilibrium. The labor market fails to recognize the contemporary social, economic and political problems of a heterogeneous society, and what looks like involuntary unemployment is involuntary unemployment.

Trade Unionism

Trade unionism or the theory of collective bargaining is another factor that determines the performance of wages in a labor market. There is a relationship between collective bargaining and nominal wages. In periods of expansion, employers might be willing to agree to substantial advances in wage rates if they were confident that, when prosperity ended, they would be able to cancel them. They know, however, that they will have to go through elaborate processes to cancel them and that their workers will put up a strong rear-guard action. In periods of depression, wage-earners, for precisely similar reasons, might be ready to make concessions if it were not for the difficulty that they foresee in getting them cancelled when time improved. A widespread desire for safety first helps to make wage rates sticky.

Equilibrium Theory

The controversies over the theory of unemployment will remain the same. However, if the labor market is imperfect, if wages are sticky, and they respond to nontraditional signals, then there is a role for an effective public policy. If the labor market is operating at equilibrium, then there will be no need for unemployment public policy.

In an economic system where there is true competition among workers, then the only possible equilibrium position will be at full employment. The equilibrium theorists seem to have the right answers, but they were mere assumptions that need to be proved. A reasonable theory of unemployment policy needs to be based on a reasonable theory of contemporary heterogeneous society.

FEDERAL GOVERNMENT POLICIES DESIGNED TO SOLVE UNEMPLOYMENT PROBLEMS 1933–1988

There have been several federal government policies for addressing unemployment problems. This study is concerned primarily with government programs designed to help the unemployed either by treating the symptoms of unemployment or by providing jobs or training. The focus, therefore, is on government policies that affect the unemployed, rather than broader policies and strategies that directly or indirectly affect the overall level of unemployment.

Since the Great Depression of the 1930s, there has not been a shortage of government strategies for helping the jobless. Franklin D. Roosevelt, with his New Deal policy, pumped billions of dollars into temporary employment programs to help those affected by the depression. The policy was designed to provide training programs for unemployed low-income individuals. During this period of depression, policymakers proposed and passed into law several measures to aid the unemployed.

Direct and indirect federal government strategies for aiding the unemployed go back to the 1930s. Before the Great Depression, unemployment was not seen as a federal government problem. There has been a dramatic shift and expansion of the federal government policy to assist the jobless since the Great Depression. Government intervention has been intense and extensive during some periods of high unemployment and limited at other times of economic growth. The United States government involvement in aiding the unemployed was intensified during the domestic and global economic crisis of the 1930s, and this remedial action resulted from the election of Franklin D. Roosevelt and a Congress that was committed to government intervention. With one out of every four people out of job, President Roosevelt's emergency relief act sailed through Congress, providing temporary employment, short-term funds, and other humanitarian assistance for the unemployed.

President Roosevelt and Congress were sympathetic to the plight of the jobless; they introduced unprecedented measures to create jobs. Each New

Deal job program had a common objective; to assist the unemployed while at the same time to provide public benefits. The Public Works Administration, for example, received over $3 billion and created thousands of jobs for building highways, dams, roads, public buildings, and other public works projects. The Works Progress Administration hired over 8 million workers and received over $11 billion.[12]

Policymakers designed programs that maintained consumer demands, alleviate human suffering, and quiet the social unrest of the highest unemployment recorded in the history of the United States. Public works programs were developed to assist jobless workers who were willing and able to work. Roosevelt's New Deal policies proved to the American people that government could successfully create useful jobs during periods of depression and high unemployment.

There are different categories of government assistance for the unemployed. They are grouped into two main unemployment programs: cyclical unemployment programs and structural unemployment programs. Cyclical unemployment programs are for people who are temporarily unemployed due to declining business activities. Structural unemployment programs are for people who suffer from chronic unemployment due to changes in demand for their skills in the labor market. The idea behind the cyclical unemployment programs is that the government should help the unemployed maintain their standard of living during economic downturns until they are able to find work. Policymakers argue that government should provide temporary help to the unemployed to prevent them from losing their homes, cars, and their possessions.

Cyclical Unemployment Program

There are two categories of cyclical unemployment programs: income support and job-creation programs. The income support provides temporary income for the unemployed worker. The major income support program is the unemployment insurance program. This system is funded by the contributions made by the employer, state revenues, and by federal grants and loans to state governments. Job-creation measures are another instrument for fighting cyclical unemployment. Here, the federal government bears the cost of temporary jobs in the state and local governments. It is more effective and efficient to use the unemployed to improve public works and services than to allow them to sit idle and collect unemployment benefits.

Structural Unemployment Programs

The rationale for structural unemployment programs is that the chronically unemployed will need government job training assistance to be more competitive in the labor market. The structural unemployment programs are designed to aid the chronically unemployed acquire job skills that allow them to gain employment. The primary beneficiaries of structural unemployment programs are the disadvantaged groups. This includes minorities, low-income groups, and people with little or no education, training or work experience. Some displaced workers also benefit from these programs. Due to the mismatch between the structurally unemployed skills and the skills desired by employers, policymakers believe that government should provide training programs, offer remedial assistance and sponsor employers' incentive programs to employ the disadvantaged groups. The theory behind such policy is that assistance for the structurally unemployed will reduce the cost of federal aid for the unemployed and other government income-transfer programs.

Unemployment insurance is a major legacy of the Great Depression public policy. The national unemployment insurance system has continued for years without interruption while other temporary job programs come and go, while some of them generated a great deal of controversy. The unemployment insurance is deeply imbedded in the national welfare system, just like health care for the elderly and the social security pension. It is among the very few government programs that politicians are reluctant to touch, excepting in the case of expanding the benefits to include more people.

Government spending on unemployment insurance fluctuates with the change in economic conditions. The cost of unemployment insurance grows as the duration and amount of benefits increase. The unemployment insurance is sometimes called middle-class welfare because its beneficiaries are working class people with stable employment records. To receive the unemployment benefits, they are required to prove that they are waiting to be recalled to a regular job or that they are looking for jobs in their occupational field.

Unlike the public assistance for low-income people, unemployment insurance has no expectation that limits it to only poor people that need assistance. Many Americans believe that the unemployment insurance is a fair program because everyone is entitled to the unemployment check. Despite the enormous scope and costs of unemployment insurance, fewer than half of the unemployed workers receive the benefits. Part-time workers, self-employed workers, temporary workers and those who used up their benefits do not receive the unemployment insurance check.

During the early 1960s, the federal government programs for unemployment took a dramatic turn when President Kennedy and a Democratic Congress found a compelling reason to set up temporary job programs. The Public Works Acceleration Act of 1962 was enacted, authorizing about one billion dollars for building and maintaining projects in communities experiencing high levels of chronic unemployment. This Act was given priority by the government. The Area Redevelopment Act of 1961 created job training and industrial revitalization programs for poor communities and states. The Manpower Development and Training Act of 1962 assists workers, who lost their jobs because of automation, through retraining to obtain jobs.

President Johnson's War on Poverty provided a great boost for unemployment programs. New unemployment programs were created as the categories of the structurally unemployed workforce were being defined. Politicians and policymakers jumped on the bandwagons of seeing employment-training programs as a potential remedy for breaking the culture of poverty. National policymakers saw job training as the effective program to combine with health, education, and social services to help people who are chronically unemployed escape indefinite public assistance. During the 1960s, several employment and training programs were created by the federal government and administered by public and private organizations. The two main legislative Acts, the Manpower Development and Training Act and Economic Opportunity Act, provided over 12 different programs for high school dropouts, inner city youths, delinquents, welfare recipients, and older workers. These programs helped disadvantaged groups with limited education, skills and job experience.

Unlike the unemployment insurance or public work projects that benefit a wide range of unemployed workers, War on Poverty programs were targeted towards the poor, minorities, and people in depressed communities and states. These employment and training programs created some controversies during the 1960s. The beneficiaries of the War on Poverty program made no financial contribution to these programs; many were not even taxpayers, while others had never worked before. Some conservatives argued that the War on Poverty rewarded people who do not merit it and whose chronic unemployment was a result of their own making. The various organizations and agencies that administered the War on Poverty programs also contributed to the controversies.

President Johnson and the democratically-controlled Congress could not trust the ability and the commitment of the state and local governments to serve poor people and minorities; new channels were created to distribute the funds to the target groups. The federal government was channeling funds to community-based agencies directly, bypassing state and local government officials. Some of the community groups employed political activists who criticized the local government officials. In some cases, the federal government funds helped to underwrite protests by the poor and minorities against the policies and practices of local and state governments. National policymakers and politicians reacted negatively to such development. Governors, mayors, county executives and other local officials demanded far more control over the planning and implementation of the War on Poverty policy.

Despite the negative reaction, employment and training programs for the chronically unemployed and poor people continued uninterrupted throughout the Johnson's era. Johnson's administration reduced the spending on training programs for the long-term unemployed and poor Americans significantly less than the spending for job-creating programs or unemployment insurance. In the 1960s, annual spending was one billion dollars for job training for the disadvantaged workers and about two billion annually in the 1970s.

The Comprehensive Employment and Training Act (CETA)

President Richard Nixon signed the Comprehensive Employment and Training Act (CETA) into law in December of 1973. CETA was the cornerstone of the nation's manpower policy and was designed to provide job training and employment opportunities to the unemployed, underemployed and economically disadvantaged individuals. CETA combined several existing categorical manpower programs into a single block grant program. It also transferred the management of these programs from the federal government to the local governments. The Nixon administration opposed the idea of a big centralized government and favored the CETA prime sponsor system as the most effective process to provide employment and training services to the disadvantaged and unemployed people. The prime sponsor system is made up of units of local government with a population of 100,000 or more who contract with the federal government to manage CETA programs at the local government level. In its brief history, from 1973 to 1983, CETA served millions of Americans and helped them to obtain productive and useful careers.

The enactment of CETA coincided with the recession of the early 1970s when the unemployment rate was 9 percent. It was designed to create jobs, help the poor, reduce the high school drop out rate, reduce juvenile delinquency, and convert welfare recipients into workers and to conserve natural resources. All of these worthwhile socials goals were the intent of the CETA. There was one concern, and that was decentralization. Based on historical facts, there was skepticism that local government politicians did not have the experience or were not willing to help the economically disadvantaged. Decentralization adversely affected the participation of youths, minorities, and private organizations.

CETA transformed federal government employment and training programs, and transferred operation from the federal to state and local governments. CETA was the main mechanism for United States unemployment public policy from 1973 to 1983.

It was one of the employment programs that effectively provided steady employment to the chronically unemployed. Its public service employment program was the centerpiece of federal government's role in stimulating employment activities; CETA was a good program that sought to help the long-term unemployed obtain jobs. From 1973 to 1983, CETA accounted for virtually all the discretionary expenditures and for a large amount of total expenditure for unemployment programs.

During the ten years of its existence, CETA experienced a lot of changes as over 60 billion were spent to train millions of unemployed workers and millions of temporary jobs were created. In the first year of CETA, the total spending was $3.7 billion on training and jobs programs. Two years later, the spending doubled, and it tripled in 1979. By 1982, the Reagan administration reduced it to its original level (See Table 3.1). The fluctuation in the level of expenditure reflects the federal government's change in employment policy objectives. CETA changed dramatically during its life span as a result of the fluctuation. Public service employment programs were added in 1974 and 1977, modified in 1978, and eliminated by Reagan in 1981.

The entire program went through comprehensive reform by 1982. Originally, CETA's main objective was to train the chronically unemployed for private sector jobs. Later, the federal government added emergency job components onto CETA to counter the effects of the 1974–1975 recession. Over the next few years, CETA jumped from providing about 100,000 jobs to providing about 1,000,000 jobs by 1979.[13]

Public Service Employment (PSE) program was large and visible but was only part of the job-creating measures of CETA. In fact, public service and public works employment programs were enacted and abolished with frequent changes sometimes making it difficult to distinguish between old and new programs. Between 1971 and 1973, the cost of temporary employment programs was about $4 billion annually. During President Carter's administration, the cost of temporary jobs programs ballooned to an average of $13 billion per year. In CETA's ten-year history, more money was channeled to employment creation than ever before in the history of federal government employment policy.

In 1978, additional authorization was given to CETA involving the private sector. The private sector initiative program established private industry councils, made up primarily of people in business, to advise local employment and training agencies on how to improve the effectiveness of the operations and programs. Targeted Jobs Tax Credit of 1978 was designed to help the chronically unemployed, and it was also a part of new private sector initiative programs. The program rewarded employers with tax credit for hiring chronically unemployed citizens who fell into any one of the categories of need. The categories of unemployed targeted in the legislation were: Vietnam-era veterans,

Table 3.1. Appropriations for CETA
Fiscal Years 1975 to 1983 (in millions of dollars)

	1975	1976	1977	1978	1979	1980	1981	1982	1983
Total	3,743	6,339	8,053	8,125	10,290	8,128	7,740	3,895	3,990
Comprehensive Training	1,819	2,302	2,481	2,268	2,361	2,922	2,821	1,925	2,409
Special Youth	174	814	1,274	417	1,238	1,492	1,636	1,204	622
Summer Youth	473	528	595	756	785	609	839	766	824
Public Service Employment	1,275	3,325	3,703	4,684	5,905	3,105	2,444	0	0
Dislocated Workers	0	0	0	0	0	0	0	0	135

Sources: Employment and Training Administration, U.S. Department of Labor, and *Budget of the United States.*

low-income youths, ex-convicts, public assistance recipients, and those re-
ferred by vocational rehabilitation agencies. The tax credit gave employers a
50 percent credit against their federal tax obligations for the first $600 of wage
target group employees during their first year of employment, and 25 percent
credit on the first $6,000 of their second year's wages.

After Ronald Reagan's election in 1980, he started dismantling CETA.
First, he terminated CETA's public service employment program. Reagan
eliminated temporary job-creation programs from the 1982 budget. In about
a year, however, Congress enacted once again public works employment program, the Transportation Assistance Act of 1982 and, in 1983, a $4.6 billion
employment-creating program. The Reagan administration even jeopardized
the less controversial training program during the first two years in office.

CETA was amended eight times. The Comprehensive Employment and
Training Act Amendments of 1978 reauthorized CETA for another 4 years. The
provision added new programs and changed CETA. It focused mainly on public service employment (PSE) programs. The Carter administration proved that
the PSE could be used to reduce cyclical unemployment. In one year, the participants grew from 190,000 to 753,000.[14] The Carter administration demonstrated that the PSE could be a useful countercyclical program when combined
with an automatic triggering process to avoid delay, providing strong financial
support for program stability, planning and continuity, and also more flexibility
to enable the local officials to design programs to suit their local needs.

CETA and Federalism

The activities of the United States Department of Labor and Congress
changed the complex intergovernmental relationships between the CETA
prime sponsors. The actions of Congress and DOL in managing CETA programs seemed to be inconsistent and lacked continuity. Often Congress
changed its legislative priorities, from categorical to decentralized, decatego-
rized programs, from comprehensive programs to recategorized programs
and DOL's actions were inconsistent because both DOL and Congress
stressed different goals at different times. These changes were as a result of
changing political and economic conditions such as change in president,
change in the coalitions within Congress supporting employment and training
legislation and also the discretionary use of any power given to both national
and regional DOL officials.

CETA rules and regulations gave states more responsibility for planning
and coordinating statewide activities of manpower services and for monitoring local prime sponsors' CETA programs. States were grappling with the
same administrative problems that confronted local prime sponsors, which
were that of uncertainties and difficulties of developing and implementing

statewide coordination of the CETA programs. CETA provisions allowed each state to create a State Manpower Services Council (SMSC), which was composed of citizens and representatives of community groups, state agencies, and local government. The role of SMSC was to review the annual plans of local prime sponsors, to monitor program operations, and to make recommendations for improving coordination between prime sponsors and state agencies. The SMSC helped distribute the so-called four percent funds, also known as the governors' discretionary funds. The discretionary funds were used to finance state agency manpower programs and for providing services to special participant groups such as minorities, women, youths and handicapped. CETA provided extra funds for vocational education purposes. Six percent of the amount of the basic training title went to the governors to be used by prime sponsors for vocational education. Each state department of education and SMSC was involved in deciding how the prime sponsors would use the funds.

The essence of intergovernmental relations is the relative influence of different levels of government in developing and implementing public policy. The major characteristic of intergovernmental relations is change and the federal government is often the source of the change. The main trends of federalism in the employment and training policy involved the federal government's role, and an increasing role for the state and local governments. The manpower programs of the 1960s were characterized by a very strong federal government role. In the 1970s, state and local governments acquired a significant new role. The national government's role shifted from substance to procedure, but remained the dominant role.

Federalism in action creates both confusion and opportunities in the implementation of CETA. Federalism had a mixed impact on the CETA implementation process. The Department of Labor's effectiveness was impeded by some factors. It shifted from goal to goal. Congress often changed its economic objectives, which caused the DOL to change its priorities. DOL was confused and uncertain about how to achieve certain program objectives, in particular, decategorization and private sector participation. There was competition among goals that actions taken to promote one goal may adversely affect another goal.

But on the other hand, some of the state and local program officials were skillful, efficient, and effective. The virtue of CETA and federalism was that the decentralization approach to employment and training gave the local operations the freedom to experiment and fit their programs to the needs of local areas. Overall, CETA produced more benefits in the training and employment arena than its predecessors' manpower policies.

CETA participation had positive and lasting economic benefits for participants. CETA also had a favorable return on public involvement from a societal point of view. In spite of the good performance of CETA, its fate was decided by 1981–1982. CETA had many positive accomplishments, but they were not effectively communicated nor was it sufficient to influence the political decision to terminate CETA. CETA was generally or significantly successful in many ways, with regards to achieving various program objectives. CETA failed to sell itself and its accomplishments politically.

The Death of Public Service Employment (PSE)

Between March and September 1981, following Reagan's instructions, the Labor Department froze hiring nationwide and instructed state and local governments to terminate over 300,000 Public Service Employment (PSE) positions. The Department of Labor promised that it would help PSE jobholders obtain full-time-unsubsidized employment. DOL required the whole employment and training system—from the state employment service offices to private industry councils—to make placement of public service employees into permanent jobs the highest priority.

In 1978, the federal government program funded over 725,000 jobs nationwide. By 1981, the CETA participants dropped to about 300,000 and in 1982, CETA was terminated. The sudden death of PSE was as a result of the Reagan administration's cutback policy. Most of the unabsorbed federally subsidized employees were left unemployed and were qualified to receive federal government assistance including unemployment insurance, food stamps, and welfare. Studies by the General Accounting Office indicated that the result of the re-employment effort was a failure. The Labor Department reported in September 1981 that only about 38 percent of the 300,000 employees that were laid-off were re-employed nationwide.[15] The result of the re-employment was pathetic, considering the nature of post-program PSE employment success. Of those who were re-employed, only about half gained full-time permanent employment, the remaining half obtained temporary and part-time positions.[16]

The state and local governments who had to absorb the PSE employees into their payrolls realized the immediate effect of the PSE death and it was too costly. Big cities with high levels of disadvantaged groups were hardest hit. Reductions took pace in all governmental levels and departments. Social services, public works, parks and recreation, and health services suffered the most cutbacks. The social services eliminated or reduced typically included child and adult day care, legal services for the poor, and aid to the disabled and elderly. Local governments reported delays in scheduled maintenance of roads, bridges and other pubic facilities.

Congressional Budget Office (CBO) estimated that, in 1981, the savings in direct federal spending due to the termination of PSE decreased to about 29 percent because of losses in tax revenues and increased federal government spending in income transfer programs.[17] The Eagleton Institute of Politics at Rutgers University calculated the indirect cost of laying off PSE workers in New Jersey. For the first year of eliminating PSE, it cost $25 million in additional payments to people who could not obtain other jobs. Over $20 million were in unemployment insurance payments. The rest was in food stamps and public assistance. The elimination of PSE also reduced the federal and state government tax revenues by about $15 million during the first year.[18] The cost of killing PSE was high.

Public Service Employment (PSE) became one of the first casualties of the Reagan Revolution. In January of 1982, the president presented to Congress the fiscal year 1983 budget. The budget proposed to restructure training programs completely, lumping them into a block grant to the states and cutting funding by two-thirds from their 1981 level—the last Carter budget. The Reagan administration also proposed to cut off community service employment for the elderly and summer jobs for inner-city youths and to decrease spending for the Job Corps. The president's budget stressed a broader economic agenda, rather than direct government spending, as the solution to unemployment problems.

The administration predicted that their strategy of cutting taxes and budget would result in a lower unemployment rate in 1982. Reagan's 1982 budget predicted an average rate of 7.2 percent for fiscal year 1983. The proposed 1983 budget adjusted that prediction upward to 8.9 percent but anticipated a gradual decline in unemployment to 7.1 percent in fiscal year 1984, 6.4 percent in fiscal year 1985, and 5.8 percent in fiscal year 1986. Instead of declining, unemployment shot upward during 1982 from 8.6 percent in January to 10.8 percent in December, for an annual average of 9.7 percent. The national economy plunged into a deep recession and experienced the highest unemployment since the Great Depression. Towards the end of 1982, Congress put heavy pressure on the president to abandon his opposition to federal government job creation and training programs. On October 13, 1982, President Reagan signed the Job Training Partnership Act (JTPA) to replace the Comprehensive Employment Training Act (CETA).

Job Training Partnership Act (JTPA)

Reagan signed Job Training Partnership ACT (JTPA) into law on October 13, 1982. The law replaced CETA and was designed to encourage business to work together with state and local governments to train disadvantaged or dislocated workers for employment in the private sector (See Table 3.2). Eventually, Reagan created its own federal job-training program by changing CETA's operation and name to the Job Training Partnership Act (JTPA).

Table 3.2. Key Provisions of JTPA Compared with CETA

	The Job Training Partnership Act (October 1983-present)	CETA (April 1979 to September 1983)
Target groups	Low-income and long-term unemployed; 60 percent adult. 40 percent youth-, 10 percent "window" for the nonpoor; includes dislocated workers.	Low-income and long-term unemployed; no specific program for dislocated workers.
Program activities and restrictions	On-the-job training, classroom training, and other activities that lead to jobs in the private sector; 70 percent of funds must go for training; restrictions on the use of funds for work experience; public service jobs prohibited; payment of stipends or wages to trainees restricted.	Work experience, on-the-job training, classroom training, supportive services, remedial education; restrictions on the use funds to pay wages or stipends to program enrollees.
State role governor	Responsible for overall program coordination and monitoring of state and local programs; approves or disapproves local plans; deter mines the areas that will deliver local programs; administers state level programs for older workers, dislocated workers; appoints state advisory council.	Administers programs in areas failing outside CETA prime sponsorships; a(ministers special programs; appoints statewide advisory council.
Service delivery areas	Units of local government partnerships with PICs, with a population over 200,000 or serving a substantial area of the labor market.	Units of local government with a population of 100,000, remainder in balance of state.
Local program management	PICs composed of representatives from the private sector, as the majority partner; form labor, education, and other groups; appointed by local elected officials; plans must be approved jointly by PICs and local elected officials.	Chief elected official of the local political jurisdiction; local advisory councils, appointed by elected officials, offer advice but do not approve or disapprove plans.
Federal role	Promulgation of national performance standards; management of research and demonstration projects; management of national programs for Indians, migrant workers, the Job Corps.	Principal responsibility for oversight of the system, including review and assessment of activities and delivery of technical assistance research and demonstration projects management of national programs for Indians, migrant workers, youth, the Job Corps, and other programs.

Source: Employment and Training Administration, U. S. Department of Labor

Employment and training programs would not have survived if it were not for the extremely high unemployment rates in 1982. JTPA focused on skill training and private sector job placement in efforts to help the structurally unemployed. It excluded public sector jobs, revised program guidelines, and shifted major administrative responsibility from local and state government to a shared power arrangement between state, local governments, and private sector. Employers receive tax credits for hiring chronically unemployed and disadvantaged workers under the targeted job tax credit. Reagan administration's dismantling of CETA had a profound effect on job training and employment-creating measures.

Job Training Partnership Act of 1982 was developed to train the disadvantaged for work or better jobs. It targeted the economically disadvantaged but its emphasis was on efficiency in the operation of the program, and performance standards were developed. Local Private Industrial Councils (PICs) operates the program and to involve local business in program training. JTPA program structure resulted in creaming of participants to the exclusion of the most disadvantaged workers. "We find that racial and welfare targets are met, but that the most able among those groups are chosen for help. We also find some evidence of channeling. The most disadvantaged groups are less likely to receive the most successful type of training—on the job training."[19] President Reagan contrasted JTPA program with the CETA program:

> This is not another make-work dead end bureaucratic boondoggle. This program will train more than one million Americans every year in skills they can market where they live. It'll make a difference on Main Street. It'll provide help, bring hope, and encourage self-reliance and personal initiative. ....State and local government officials, business and labor leaders, and other members of the private industry councils. Local people will decide at the grassroots level what opportunities are available in their communities and then match real jobs with needed skills.[20]

Reagan's New Federalism was significantly different from Nixon's Federalism. Reagan's Federalism provided the states with more power in managing manpower programs and allowed the federal government to play a lesser role in administering employment programs. Reagan administration preferred the use of block grants rather than categorical grants for employment programs. Reagan's public policy was based on the concept of reducing federal funding for social programs. Nixon accepted federalism as a means of facilitating the implementation of social programs, but Reagan waged a comprehensive assault on the intergovernmental dimensions of public-sector activism.

Unlike CETA, which was overseen mostly by government officials, JTPA was supervised by private sector members who were appointed by local elected officials to serve on the Private Industry Councils (PICs). JTPA's primary goal was to train individuals for private sector jobs. Short-term public sector jobs were abolished, and the receiving of stipends or other income support to program participants was sharply curtailed. Reagan had opposed federal government involvement in job training programs since he came to office as a result; he switched to JTPA to replace CETA.

JTPA might not have passed had it not been for the 10 percent unemployment rate. The content of JTPA provisions was designed during a protracted debate about the accomplishments and failures of CETA. The federal government's job bill was debated over the landscape of public opinion, the national media, and national election in 1982. Finally, JTPA emerged from a less visible battle among members of the employment and training subgovernment. What were the impacts of the Reagan administration's job bill? Was it a significant improvement over CETA? Or did it hurt the people it was designed to help?

JTPA: Political Images, Myths, and Ideologies

The policy provisions in JTPA were more of political images, myths, and ideologies held by the Reagan administration and the Republicans. The new policy approaches adopted in JTPA—increased private sector involvement, state government management; training instead of income-maintenance was as a result of the administration's perceptions of CETA, and the belief that private sector initiatives and new federalism could help solve the unemployment problem. In the case of private sector involvement, the JTPA's key proponents argued that private sector participation was excluded from CETA training programs, that private sector job placements were inadequate, and that CETA's experiment with private sector initiative program was not a success. JTPA's supporters were convinced that the prime sponsor systems were inefficient and corrupt. The argument on private sector involvement was based on the Republicans conservative ideology.

The Reagan administration's elimination of stipends for short-term work experience and the emphasis on training were also based on images and political ideology. The elimination of stipends was based on the idea of changing job training from being a social service program to more involvement by the private sector. The legislation's key proponents argued that the balance between helping the jobless and satisfying the employer had tipped too far on the side of providing temporary income support.

Republicans persuaded Congress to reduce the stipends for the unemployed; they argued that more people could be enrolled in a job-training program for less money. President Reagan's New Federalism placed more responsibility for federal job training programs at the state and local levels. The administration argued that states should administer training measures because the states were already administering similar programs such as education, economic development, and public assistance. JTPA provisions were designed by the framers' perception of what was wrong with federal job training programs and the Reagan administration's political ideology. Reagan succeeded in having his political agenda and philosophy incorporated into the new law. A major amendment of the Job Training Partnership Act was added in 1982. The JTPA was amended in 1986 and the Dislocated Worker Program was amended in 1988.

JTPA authorized specific categorical programs rather than providing unrestricted block grants to state and local jurisdictions. The Title II-A program authorized training and related services to economically disadvantaged youth and adults; Title II-B continued the summer youth program, Title III authorized training for dislocated workers, and Title IV authorized national programs. In addition to being responsible for the Title III Dislocated Worker Program, states were given considerable oversight and monitoring responsibilities.

The Title II programs were to be conducted through local Service Delivery Areas (SDAs) similar to the prime sponsors in CETA. Designation of SDAs was a responsibility of the governor, but governors were required to approve requests from local governments with a population of 200,000 or more. Under CETA, designation of prime sponsors was the responsibility of the Secretary of Labor, and the population cut-off was 100,000. The intent of increasing the population cut-off was to reduce the number of local governments running programs, but JTPA did not include a provision for balance-of-state SDAs, so the number of SDAs actually increased from about 450 to over 600. Title II funds were distributed to the SDAs based on formulas using the number of unemployed and the size of the low-income population. The Title II-A program was to provide training and related services for economically disadvantaged youth and adults. States were required to distribute 78 percent of the Title II-A allocation to the SDAs and the remaining 22 percent was for the following set-asides: eight percent for coordination between JTPA and education programs; six percent for performance awards to SDAs for enrolling the hard-to-serve; three percent for programs for older workers, and five percent for state administration. The major activities provided were classroom training, basic skills and vocational, on-the-job training, job search assistance. Work experience was limited because SDAs could not spend more than 30 percent of their funds on administration, allowance, and support services.

Private Industry Councils (PICs) were established under CETA in 1978, but they were assigned more responsibility under JTPA. The chief elected officials in the SDAs appointed PIC members. At least 51 percent of the PIC members and the chairperson were to be from the private sector and selected from nominations made by a general purpose business organization such as the chamber of commerce. Other PIC members were to represent interest groups such as the employment agencies, organized labor, and local educational institutions. The PICs were given the authority to operate the programs or serve as an advisory body. The Title II-A program was targeted for the economically disadvantaged: at least 90 percent of the Title II-A participants were required to be economically disadvantaged, defined in terms of low income over the six-month period prior to entry, participation in a cash welfare program or food stamps, or being a foster child or disabled and poor. Ten percent of the participants were permitted to exceed the income cut-offs if they faced other barriers to employment, but SDAs used this provision as audit insurance. SDAs were generally required to spend 40 percent of their Title II-A allocation on youths under age 22, and school drop-outs, and welfare recipients were to be served in proportion to their prevalence in the eligible population.

JTPA Title II-B continued the summer youth employment and training program. The program was established primarily for youths, ages 16 to 21, but 14- and 15-year olds were eligible if designated in the SDA's annual plan. Initially, the Title II-B program was similar to the CETA youth summer jobs program. In 1986, concern that economically disadvantaged youths needed to improve their basic skills as well as gain work experience led to amendments requiring that participants have their reading and math skills assessed and that local plans explain how participants would be provided with basic and remedial education. Title III provided training and job search assistance to dislocated workers. Originally, Title III was entirely a state-level program and states had to match the funding on a dollar-for-dollar basis. The matching requirement was reduced by 10 percent for each percentage point that the state could count 50 percent of its contributions for unemployment insurance and its contributions for other training programs for the participants.

Congressional interest in dislocated workers remained strong after the passage of JTPA. Congress was concerned about whether the original Title III program provided the best distribution of funds across and within states, whether dislocated workers received appropriate services, and whether workers whose job losses resulted from mass lay-offs and plant closings were receiving enough service, and whether the services they received were enacted in the summer of 1988. The Worker Adjustment and Retraining Notification Act (WARN), enacted in July 1988, required employers in certain circumstances to provide sixty days' advance notice to workers and the state dislocated worker unit in the event of a mass lay-off or plant closing. In August 1988, subpart D of the Omnibus Trade and Competitiveness Act included the Economic Dislocation and Work Adjustment Assistance Act (EDWAA), which modified the JTPA Title III program.

A major new feature in EDWAA was the allocation of funds to substate areas. Governors could retain up to 40 percent of the state's allocation for statewide activities, but the remaining 60 percent had to be allocated to substate areas. The governor could withhold up to 10 percent of the funds so long as they were distributed by a formula based on need within nine months. Governors are to develop a substate allocation formula based on insured unemployment data, unemployment concentrations, plant closings, and mass lay-off data, declining industries data, farmer-rancher economic hardship data, and long-term unemployment data. Other factors could be added at the governor's discretion. The JTPA Title II-A performance standards system illustrates one method by which the federal government could influence state and local governments in JTPA without necessarily amending the legislation. JTPA requires the Department of Labor to issue performance standards, and permits governors to prescribe variations within parameters established by the Secretary based on economic, geographic, and demographic factors in the state. The language in the statute regarding performance standards is somewhat confusing, and several authors have concluded that the JTPA performance standards system does not meet the statutory intent of measuring gains due to participating in the program. The performance standards system permits financial rewards to SDAs that exceed the standards and potential sanctions, including loss of the right to operate the program for SDAs that fail to meet them.

JTPA statute gave the Department of Labor authority to issue numerical standards for outcomes of interest, for example, the proportion of participants employed thirteen weeks after termination, and the states have the authority to vary expected performance depending on economic conditions, characteristics of the population served, and program activities. The use of numerical standards without adjusting for characteristics of the population served results in incentives to cream, which means the, selection of those who are least disadvantaged, and serving those with the best chance of succeeding without participating in JTPA. In an effort to hold SDAs harmless for enrolling participants who are hard to place, the Department of Labor developed and updated regression models that attempt to account for differences in participant characteristics and economic conditions among SDAs. As the performance standards system became more accepted and understood by states and SDAs, the Department of Labor used the performance standard system to encourage the states and SDAs to administer the program in accordance with national policy. In the early years of JTPA, states were free to minimize the importance of the national standards by adding their own performance measures and giving little or no weight to the national standards.

Congress framed the Job Training Partnership Act to help the economically disadvantaged, but the Labor Department and Congress were concerned that state and local officials were using it to help people who need it the least. JTPA was designed to emphasize program outcomes which meant that the private contractors were paid based on their performance in placing JTPA program participants in jobs, and the wages in those jobs, as well as ensuring that PICs met performance standards. The federal role in JTPA was peripheral. Jeff Faux[21] stated, "In the JTPA, there is an obsession with very, very short-term goals, placing people very quickly in jobs they would have gotten anyway." Faux concluded, "The legislative language encourages you, by virtue of the way the program measures success, to cream like crazy and skew the funding towards the relatively advantaged, because you get your money based upon your successes in transitioning workers into jobs." Other critics have noted:

> A lack of direction in JTPA has undermined the program in part because it was established to serve conflicting constituencies. Federal job training efforts have suffered from schizophrenia in purpose, with nobody defining how to sort conflicts. ....the program served advocates of economic development who argued that the needs of disadvantaged and dislocated workers are best met through building the economic base.[22]

Reagan administration wiped the slate clean by changing the employment training law's name to JTPA and modifying its management structure. It created some new problems, solved a few, and ignored some. JTPA did not pay sufficient attention to the needs of the most economically disadvantaged. JTPA promotes creaming which results in federal dollars being poorly invested in training people who could obtain employment without federal programs, while those who the federal assistance program was designed for, because they are chronically unemployed, and remain on public welfare, food stamps, and other forms of dependency. JTPA was clearly inefficient because it was in favor of helping employers select those who were least disadvantaged. The enactment of the JTPA did not solve the basic problem facing employment and training administrators. How can the poor, minority, youths, women and long term unemployed be helped to become self-sufficient, productive members of the labor force? JTPA has not proven to be better than CETA for helping the long-term unemployed and low-income people to obtain employment.

NOTES

1. Stephen K. Bailey, *Congress Makes a Law* (New York: Columbia University Press, 1980) 3.
2. Gallup Poll Report (September 1982): 6–7.

3. Isabel V. Sawhill, "Rethinking Employment Policy" in *Rethinking Employment Policy*, ed. Lee Bawden and Felicity Skidmore (Washington, D.C.: Urban Institute Press, 1989), 9.

4. William H. Beveridge, *Full Employment in a Free Society* (London: Allen and Unwin, 1944), 18.

5. "United States Labor Department's Annual Survey on Work and Joblessness" in *National Journal* (20 August 1983): 1754.

6. Donald C. Baumer and Carl Van Horn, *The Politics of Unemployment* (Washington, DC, Congressional Quarterly, 1985) 2.

7. Wayne J. Howe, "Education and Demographics: How Do They Affect Unemployment Rates?" *Monthly Labor Review* (January 1988): 3.

8. Sar A. Levitan, Garth L. Mangum and Ray Marshall, *Human Resources and Labor Markets* (New York: Harper and Row, 1981), 35–39.

9. Wayne J. Howe, "Education and Demographics: How Do They Affect Unemployment Rates?" *Monthly Labor Review* (January 1988) 8.

10. Bureau of Labor Statistics, "Employment Situation January 1984," *News* (United States Department of Labor, 3 February 1984): 84.

11. James Kearl and others, "A Confusion of Economists?" *American Economic Review* (May 1979): 28–37.

12. Arthur MacMahon and others, *The Administration of Federal Work Relief* (Chicago: Public Administration Service, 1941).

13. Grace A. Franklin and Randall B. Ripley, *CETA: Politics and Policy, 1973–1982* (Knoxville: University of Tennessee Press, 1984).

14. Ray Marshall, Selective Employment Programs and Economic Policy," *Journal of Economic Issues* (March 1984) 124.

15. General Accounting Office, *Implementation of the Phaseout of CETA Public Service Jobs* (Washington, DC: GPO. 1982) 14.

16. General Accounting Office, *Implementation*. 17.

17. Congressional Budget Office, *Effects of Eliminating Public Service Employment* (Washington, D.C.: GPO, June 1981), xi.

18. Van Horn and Raimondo, *The Impact of Reductions in Federal Aid to New Jersey* (New Brunswick, N.J.: Rutgers University Press, May 1982) 15–17.

19. Kathryn H. Anderson et al., "Mixed Signals in the Job Training Partnership Act," *Growth and Change* (Summer 1991): 32.

20. Ronald Reagan, *Public Papers of the Presidents* (Washington, D.C.: GPO, 1982), 1305.

21. Jeff Faux of Economic Policy Institute, quoted in Kirk Victor, "Helping the Haves," *National Journal,* 14 April 1980, 901.

22. Kirk Victor, "Helping the Haves," *National Journal,* 14 April 1990, 902.

Chapter Four

Fiscal Policy and Reaganomics

With the exception of Franklin D. Roosevelt, no American president in modern history can be compared to Ronald Reagan in changing the direction of the national economy. Reagan's ability to convince Congress to approve his policies for unprecedented tax and expenditure cuts surprised both his critics and supporters. In contrast, the Roosevelt New Deal policy was synonymous with government expansion, while Reagan's supply-side policy meant massive tax and expenditure cuts in almost all federal government programs except defense. Most presidents change incrementally from the existing policy. The Reagan administration was successful in shifting completely the direction of the federal government's economic policy. After the Reagan revolution, the established centrist consensus from which new administrations will deviate shifted forever the whole path of economic policy.

Ronald Reagan was elected to office as a fiscal conservative. He promised to cut taxes, government expenditures, regulation, inflation, interest rates, and unemployment. The administration's programs for implementing the campaign promises became a source of great controversy. Political scientists and economists are still studying the impact of Reaganomics. The question most frequently asked is what is supply-side policy or Reaganomics? This chapter is designed to answer the major questions about Reaganomics. It is President Ronald Reagan's fiscal policy.

Reagan arrived in the White House with a strong and distinctive social and economic ideology. FDR and LBJ were pragmatists, not ideologists and they responded to the social and economic problems they faced. The New Deal and the Great Society programs were not governed by any complex doctrine or ideology from the presidents, although their policies were called liberal. Ronald Reagan came to power with a ready-made conservative ideology.

The basic tenet of Reagan's public policy was the need to cut government expenditure and activity in managing the affairs of the national economy. Reagan often spoke of the futility of government throwing money at social problems, just like the New Deal and the Great Society programs. He believed that the money spent on social programs, such as anti-poverty programs, would be better left in the hands of the middle-class and rich as tax cuts. In that sense, they will invest these funds in the private sector, which will generate economic activities to help further commerce and industry, create jobs and reduce inflation. This is also called trickle down economic theory. Reaganomics is a mere combination of Reagan's conservative ideology and several loose sets of economic theories. This theory was based on limited past economic experiences and policies. The failures of the Keynesian economic theory in the 1970s and the Carter administration's economic programs, coupled with the frustration over federal government bureaucracy, led voters to embrace the Reagan campaign promise, and in November of 1980, they voted him into office.

SUPPLY-SIDE THEORIES AND ASSUMPTION

Reagan administration pursued supply-side management approach, which is the logical correlation of supply-side economics. Supply-side approach dominated decisions on budgeting, financial management, regulation, information policy, procurement, personnel, and program management. The approach brought to the forefront a renewed emphasis on governmental performance, a potentially lasting legacy, but failed in many ways.

Ronald Reagan's supply-side economic theory is a very important component of his approach to a responsible federal government. The administration tried to bring a distinctive and strong ideology to economic policy. Previously unpopular, but also a very important tool in economic management, supply-side theory became the cornerstone and the logical corollary to the administration's economic policy. There has been much criticism of the supply-side economics. Some well-known economists and political leaders expressed their views on the supply-side economics as just a quaky and crazy idea. In view of theses criticisms, an examination of the theoretical basis and historical origins of supply-side economics seems appropriate. This section will define the major components of the supply-side theory and relate it to the Reagan administration's fiscal policy.

A brief definition and elaboration of the essential principles of supply-side economic theory is appropriate at this point. Supply-side theory states that the amount of federal government spending and the tax burden are a drag on the national economy. The theory argues that by reducing federal government expenditures and taxes, activities in the private sector would increase revenue and will result in economic growth, and reduce unemployment and inflation; tax revenue will naturally increase the fund for general governmental services. The main line of thought that distinguishes economic theories from other theories is that human beings respond to changes in economic incentives. All things being equal, people buy fewer products if the prices are high and more if the prices are low. Supply and demand is determined by price. Consequently, when a product is taxed, there is less of it, and when a product is subsidized, the suppliers of such a product supply more.

Supply-side economic theory points out that the reason for poor performance with respect to economic growth, productivity, and high unemployment rate is high tax burden. The theory recognizes that the primary reason for this poor economic performance is that government is over-taxing workers, savings, supply output, and at the same time subsidizing consumption of social programs. Supply-side theorists argued that if you want more of a product, reduce tax on it, and if you want less of any product, reduce subsidy on it. However, the supply-siders contends that for increased activity in the economy, high productivity, increase in personal savings, and increase in output; there must be a low tax rate. The theorists also recommend that in order to reduce unemployment, the government must reduce the subsidies on unemployment.[1]

There are three basic elements of supply-side theory. First, changes in marginal tax rates are changes in relative price that will eventually affect distribution of resources and real economic growth. Changes in tax rates would consequently affect the incentives of suppliers to produce and supply goods to the market. Tax-induced relative price changes affect choices between work and leisure, consumption and savings, and market and non-market activities. Also, reductions in tax rates will result in changes in aggregate supply and real economic growth by inducing shifts from non-work to work, from consumption to savings, and from non-market to market activities. Supply-side economists view changes in tax rates as incentive changes rather than income changes.[2]

The second element of supply-side economic theory is the relationship between tax rates and output. When tax rates are near Zero, output is low because some public goods such as defense, law and order, the maintenance of roads, and primary education which are essential for markets to operate are not being provided. When these essential public goods and services are provided and economic activities increased, the availability of these public goods and services helps to increase the productive efficiency of capital and labor, and eventually, output. Although, as tax rates begin to rise, disincentives and inefficiencies associated with these higher tax rates begin to be more significant. The higher tax rates change relative prices, and the more the after-tax benefits, savings, investing, and working for taxable income decline. Then, the individual has little or no incentive to save, invest, and work. Consequently, people shift out of these activities into leisure, consumption, tax shelters and working for nontaxable income.

The relationship between the total market output and the tax rates is the primary concern of the supply-siders. The fact that changes in tax rate affects the supply of good and services means that changes in tax rate also affect tax revenues. Specifically, tax revenue is equal to the product of tax rate times the tax base.

The third element of supply-side economics is the recognition that the various relationships of tax rates changes, factor supplies, output, and tax revenues are long-term relationships. The economic elasticity becomes greater on a long-term basis. Therefore, the longer the time frame under consideration, the more effective will supply tax cuts become. Hence, supply-side theory advocates for public policies that will address long-run economic growth and policies that will solve the economic problems based on the business cycle. It emphasizes growth not stabilization. Supply-side economics theory has its origin in the classical economic theory.

ECONOMIC THEORIES

Adam Smith

It was Adam Smith who first put forth the theory, presenting a tax-related concept that completely included all the elements of supply-side theory. Smith was concerned with creation of wealth or production. Adam Smith believed that a nation was rich or poor according to its annual production of goods and services and that wealth is made up of real goods and services rather than gold. In 1776, Smith wrote a book, *An Inquiry into the Nature and Causes of the Wealth of Nations.*[3] Smith was more concerned with the aggregate supply-side of wealth rather than being concerned with the transfer of wealth as was common during the mercantilist's era. Certainly, this pervasive concern for the nature and cause of wealth and economic growth dominated all the principles of classical economics.

Adam Smith's argument is based on the simple fact that in order for a nation to increase its economic growth, it needs to pay more attention to an increase in aggregate supply and production of goods and services rather than increase in the monetary gold stock. Smith believed that increases in aggregate supply and production also mean increase in the supply of labor and capital. The Wealth of Nations emphasizes the need for incentives in eliciting increases in labor and capital. Adam Smith explained that wage increases would always increase the supply of labor. Smith explicitly pointed out that taxes on wages were absurd and destructive and that high taxes would obstruct the industry of people and also encourages underground or tax avoidance activities such as smuggling. Increases in taxes on capital and profits would promote disincentives on saving-investing activity. He stated that these disincentives would promote flight of capital and consequently adversely affect economic growth. Smith understood that changes in tax rate affect the relationships between work and nonwork, savings and consumption, market and nonmarket activity.[4]

Adam Smith clearly recognized the important relationship between taxes and supply, and production of goods and services. Smith explicitly states the intentions of his writing:

> The high duties, which have been imposed upon the importation of many different sorts of foreign goods, in order to discourage their consumption in Great Britain, have in many cases served only to encourage smuggling; and in all cases have reduced the revenue of the customs below what more moderate duties would have afforded. The saying of Dr. Swift, that in the arithmetic of the customs two and two, instead of making four, make sometimes only one, holds perfectly true with regard to such heavy duties, which never could have been imposed had not the mercantile system taught us, in many cases to employ taxation as an instrument, not of revenue, but of monopoly.[5]

Jean Baptiste Say

Supply-side economics is in many ways the re-emergence of classical economics. Jean Baptiste Say and James Mill were some of the classicists whose writings influenced supply-side economics. Say's Law is named after him and stated that goods are paid for with other goods; therefore, it is supply and production that determine the satisfaction of human wants, not the consumption.

Say contends that the encouragement of mere consumption does not benefit the economy because the difficulty lies in supplying the goods and services and not in stimulating the desire of consumption. We have seen that production alone is responsible for the availability of goods and services. Thus, the aim of good government should be to stimulate production, and the aim of bad government is to encourage consumption.[6]

Say further refined some of Adam Smith's theory. The main focus of Say's Law is that aggregate supply and production provide wealth and economic growth to a nation. In order for a nation to have more revenue, it has to produce more. Say's Law is a simple idea, people produce to consume. Industries purchasing labor depend on supply of labor. Supply or production is the ultimate means for demand, and the origin of demand lies in production. The important message of Say's Law is that government economic policy should concentrate on aggregate supply and production rather than consumption and aggregate demand. Say believed that aggregate demand would be taken care of. Consequently, to promote aggregate supply, more attention should be paid to encouraging factors of supply. The emphasis on aggregate supply is the basic factor for the creation of wealth and real economic growth.

James Mill and other classical economists supported Say. Mill agreed with Say that increases in wages would increase the supply of labor. Both Mill and Say are very much concerned with economic growth; they are advocates for tax policies that promote work effort, savings, and investment and eventually aggregate supply and production. John Stuart Mill argued that high tax rates would discourage industry by insufficiency of reward. He stated that high tax rates would discourage the incentives to save and cause both capital and labor to diminish. When tax rates reach certain levels, they should be reduced to stimulate supply of labor, capital and, consequently, aggregate supply.

John Stuart Mill argues that nations, therefore, needs not focus on consumption. There will always be demand for all goods and services, which can be produced, until the wants of those who possess the means to consume are completely satisfied, and then, production will not increase any further. Government has to be concern solely on two areas. One, to make sure that no obstacle shall exist to prevent those who have the means of producing, from employing those means as they find most for their interest. Those who have not at present the means of producing should be encourage produce. Government should have every facility afforded to producers, and allow them to acquire the means of production, and that, by becoming producers; they may be enabled to consume more.[7]

Advocates of Say's Law support all the elements of supply-side economics. Say's Law provides the essential theory for supply-side economics, and the fundamental view for most of the classical thinking on economic policy. The fundamentals of supply-side theory, therefore, became well established with the development and elaboration of Say's Law. Because of its general appeal, its emphasis on aggregate supply and economic growth, Say's Law continued to dominate economic theory until the period of the Great Depression. During this period, John Maynard Keynes attacked supply-side theory.

The Keynesian Theory

In Keynes' book, *General Theory of Employment, Interest and Money,* he explains that the cause of the Great Depression was underconsumption and that the national economic policy should be focused towards stimulating demand, through budget and monetary policies.[8] Due to the politics of the Great Depression and the New Deal, Keynes' theory became very popular. Whatever

Keynes' theory merit as a piece of analysis may be, there cannot be any doubt
that it is widely accepted as viable alternative to supply-side theory because
of the fact that its argument provided the bases of some of the strongest political preferences of a large number of modern economists.

The Keynesian approach to government policy was an outgrowth of the
deep world-wide depression and chronic unemployment of the 1930s. Keynes
attacked Say's Law by providing a critical theory, and presented a new economic theory dealing with production, employment and income. Keynes
broke the bond of the classical economic principles that said that there was
only one normal equilibrium level for the economy, which is at full employment. According to Keynes, equilibrium can exist at full employment, widespread unemployment or any level in between. He challenged the classical assumptions that unemployment was a temporary deviation from full
employment equilibrium and that economic market forces would return the
economy to full employment.[9] However, Keynes accepts some of the classi-
calist's theory as it applied to a barter economy, but stated that it did not ap-
ply in a monetary economy. Keynes did not agree with Say's Law that money
had no utility except as purchasing power. He explained that individuals save
for the sake of saving for some reasons; they substitute a demand for money
in place of a demand for goods and services. Therefore, savings do not auto-
matically flow into investment. He also challenged the notion that via market
forces, price competition would always drive surplus goods and services off
the market, that wage competition would insure jobs for the unemployed, and
that the interest rate would equilibrate the demand for and the supply of savings.[10]

Keynesian theory argues successfully that the way to stimulate employment and output growth is through expansionary fiscal policies that are to increase federal government spending and reduce taxes. The notion is that increasing government spending will subsequently increase the demand for
goods and services while lowering taxes gives people excess disposable income to spend. He points out that increase in aggregate demand could only
come from more government spending and lower taxes which will drive up
prices thereby encouraging an increase in production. Unemployment rate
would decline as output expands because more production means more labor.
Higher prices may mean higher wages. According to Keynes, reduction in
real wages increases the employment of more people, resulting in an increase
in production of commodities.[11]

Hence, massive unemployment problems could be solved by expansionary
government fiscal policies. Excessive unemployment is an indication of market failure. Thus, the situation of unemployment is typically considered to be
a sure indication that market forces are incapable of providing jobs at full employment. In order to solve such a problem of involuntary unemployment,

government must formulate appropriate intervention fiscal policy by increasing spending and reducing taxes. During the 1960s, however, many economists persuaded the government to introduce aggressive fiscal policies to stimulate economic growth. These economists believed that to solve the unemployment problem, government needed to pursue activist demand-side fiscal policies.

The 1960s and 1970s were periods of demand-side fiscal policies. Increases in federal government spending and increases in deficits occurred while the government was pursuing economic growth to reduce the unemployment rate. However, as deficits increased, so did the growth of money supply and interest rates. Increases in money supply leads to a higher interest rate, as the inflation rate goes up, the inflation premium is incorporated into the nominal or market interest rate.

During the 1970s, the existing stagflation in the economy, and both rising inflation rates and unemployment rates created discontentment with the Keynesian view of demand-side policies. As the federal government budget grew, the economy did not grow at the same rate, nor did the unemployment rate decline, and the inflation rate was rising.

In fact, Keynesian economic theory was proclaimed dead by critics during the recession of 1974–76. In 1975, the unemployment rate was 8.5 percent, the highest level of unemployment rate since the Great Depression. Federal government budget deficit was $45 billion and a soaring inflation rate. According to conventional Keynesian theory, this could not happen. The Phillips Curve, which is a basic Keynesian component, states that there is an inverse relationship between inflation and unemployment, the higher one is, the lower the other should be. However, in the 1970's both were going the same direction; up. Thus, the Keynesians were completely baffled about what policy prescription to offer for the national economic problem. The Keynesians were therefore left without anything to offer to correct the maladies of the economy. Consequently, many critics were proclaiming the death of Keynesian economics.

The conventional Keynesian activist demand-side fiscal policies, designed to stabilize the economy, was considered to be a failed policy in the 1970s. Soon, other theories of how to stabilize the economy and stimulate growth began to receive attention. Supply-side was then suggested as an alternative.

In response to this crisis in the theory of Keynes' economic policy, a new economic theory began to emerge. The focus was on economic growth, rather than on economic equilibrium or disequilibrium. The theory sees such growth arising from a free response to the economic incentives of a free market. It does retain the Keynesian macroeconomic tools for diagnostic purposes, but its main focus is conservative rather than liberal. It believes that only the private sector can bring sustained economic growth, that

the function of the public sector should not be economic growth. The new
theory described, rather cumbersomely, is not really new but would be
known as supply-side fiscal policy.

REAGANOMICS AND FEDERALISM

New Federalism

Reagan administration's supply-side fiscal policy had a pronounced effect on
intergovernmental relations. Reagan came to Washington with a strong belief
in federalism as it was originally designed by the Founding Fathers. He was
determined to define federalism in its true meaning of decentralization of
power between federal, state and local government. Reagan's primary objective was to reduce the financial and programmatic dependency of state and local governments on the federal government, through new block grants and a
mix of budgetary and administrative devices. Right from the beginning Congress challenged his constitutional authority. Critics charged that after the euphoria of the election victory, he would learn that the power status quo of
Washington establishment would block any reform proposed by his regime.
Reagan's attempt to decentralize power had a profound impact on the effective distribution of governmental services and activities on the state and local
government level. Though he did not realize all of his objectives of new federalism, he did change the status quo. During the Reagan era, state and local
government experienced a different kind of new federalism. In the 1980's,
state and local governments, with a new sense of independence from the federal government, accepted new responsibilities.

In Reagan's acceptance speech at the Republican National Convention in
Detroit, 1980, he stated that "everything that can be run more efficiently by
state and local governments we shall turn over to local governments, along
with the funding sources to pay for it."[12] The conventional wisdom had always been that the classical theory of federalism was nothing but nonsense
and no modern president will make a genuine commitment to the original federalism of dual sovereignty. Reagan was fully aware of the climate in the
country. This is the era of modern politics, he felt comfortable to carry out his
campaign promise to satisfy his voters.

According to W. Craig Stubblebine, Reagan proposed several programs for
the new federalism:[13] (1) Assumption by the federal government of full financial and administrative responsibility for Medicaid, while continuing its
responsibility for Medicare; (2) Assumption by state government of the full
cost of food stamps and of Aid to Families with Dependent Children; (3)
"Turn-back" to the state and local governments of various federal programs

in education and training, social services, transportation, community development, and revenue sharing; (4) Consolidation of various federal categorical grant programs into block grants for child welfare, rental rehabilitation, training and employment, welfare administration, vocational and adult education, education for the handicapped, and rehabilitation services; (5) Creation of a federal trust fund financed by existing federal excise taxes and the wind-fall profits tax on oil, on which the states may draw to fund substitutes for the turn-back programs. Over time, the federal taxes financing the trust fund would be eliminated, leaving the state to enact replacement levies should they so decide.

In response to opposition from various political interest groups, Reagan revised the proposal for new federalism in the following manner: (1) Food stamps would be retained at the federal level; (2) Medicaid would be broken apart with federal responsibility limited to basic coverage and the states sharing fiscal responsibility with the federal government for Long-term care and optional services; (3) Some general federal revenues would be allocated to supporting the turn-back trust fund.

Although Congress rejected most of Reagan's New Federalism proposals, the administration successfully pursued its objective through other venues.[14] This action was reflected in the decline of federal aid as a percentage of state and local revenue. In 1985, the Advisory Commission on Intergovernmental Relations stated that in 1980 federal aid was 31.7 percent of all state/local own source revenue. By 1984, it had been reduced to 23.7 percent. The level of federal aid in 1986 was about 22 percent, just about the same level it was in the 1960s. However, state and local taxes were increasing while federal revenues were declining.

Between 1981 and 1984, the federal government tax revenue declined from 13.7 percent to 11.3 percent of gross national product. During the same period, state and local revenues increased slightly from 8.3 percent of GNP to 8.8 percent. The distribution of total federal, state, and local tax revenues changed from 62.4 percent federal and 37.6 percent state and local in 1981 to 56.3 percent federal and 43.7 percent state and local in 1984.[15]

Classical Theory of Federalism

The obvious advantage of federalism is that it combines the strengths of a central government with those of regional governments. Each level of government, rather than attempting to perform all the functions of government alone, does what it can to make its own contribution. The main responsibility of central government presumably, is to stabilize the economy, by achieving the most equitable distribution of income, and providing certain public goods and services, which influence significantly the welfare of all citizens. Complementing these functions, state and local governments can provide those public goods and services that are of primary interest only to the citizens of their respective areas. It is in this context that federalism is, in economic terms, described as the best form of government.

To further explain classical theory of federalism, we need to look at two concepts: economics of scale and externalities. Economics of scale occurs when suppliers average costs per unit of output declines as a result of increase in output. The argument is that production of government goods and services should take place at the level where it can be mass-produced at a minimum cost. Economics of externalities exist when the goods and services produced by one level of producers, have a negative effect on the welfare of another level. The argument is that the activity of one level of government may have repercussions on another level of government, such as higher taxes, higher prices for goods and services, unemployment, and a low rate of investment.[16]

There is a clear distinction between the economics of scale and externality concepts of federalism. In the economics of scale justification for federalism, what is transferred to all levels of government is responsibility for funding of the production, which may be placed at any level of the government. In the economics of externality justification what is transferred to all the levels of government is the responsibility of coordinating and making joint decisions of the government programs for the best interest of all. In that sense externality responsibility is distributed fairly to all the government levels. The economics of scale and the economics of externality justification together provide support for the idea of a multiplicity of fiscal jurisdictions.

Due to the multiple subsets in the American system, optimal form of federal government means a complex layering of fiscal jurisdictions. The United States Constitution allows only two levels of government, the federal and the state governments. The governments of several states recognize the various governmental units in their regions: counties, cities, townships, school districts, and special districts. All of which are parts of a multiplicity of fiscal jurisdictions. It is debatable whether the present complex layering of fiscal jurisdictions is an optimal form of government from the classical point of view.

The reality of political decisions imposes some limit on the proliferation of fiscal jurisdictions. At the same time, the present nature of the fiscal jurisdictions is extraordinarily complex. In his definitive treatment of the new Reaganomics theory of federalism, Richard A. Musgrave notes that the view of federalism that underlies these changes is that functions of government are performed better at the state and local level than by the federal government. Citizens are essentially citizens of their respective state, with matters of defense and foreign policy delegated to the federation. He states that it should not be a federal responsibility to assure that people living in various states are provided with an adequate level of public services, nor should it be a federal responsibility to worry about the fact that various state and local governments differ greatly in tax bases and needs, and in the effort required to provide such services.[17]

Public Choice Theory of Federalism

The public choice theory of federalism states that the public will face differing costs of acquiring additional units of collective goods and services depending on the fiscal jurisdiction to which responsibility for funding and production is assigned. The citizens have a choice to assign responsibility to the public sector if it will provide goods and services at a lower cost than the private sector and also to assign responsibility to the public sector jurisdiction that provides goods and services at the lowest tax base. An understanding of the private sector tax prices helps to explain the difference between the private and public sector funding. In the private sector, competition among producers for market and resources result in equilibrium between production price and market price. Hence, in the private sector equilibrium, the resource costs are equal to the market price. By contrast, in the public sector, the tax law and revenue allocation rules differentiate the resource costs and tax prices.[18]

In the public sector, some goods and services are being provided at tax prices in excess of valuation and some goods and services are being provided at tax prices less than valuation. Voters or citizens whose valuations are less than production costs, but greater than the tax prices will want more in the quantities of goods and services they receive. On the other hand, the public whose valuations are greater than resource costs, but less than the tax prices may oppose the continuation of the goods and services.

However, it should not be assumed that decentralization is always efficient. It may be considered efficient in that it permits different fiscal jurisdictions to be responsible in providing governmental goods and services based on their particular interest. But, the significant differences in the states' tax systems affect the equitable distribution of economic resources and consequently affect efficiency in allocation. Decentralized fiscal systems, therefore, are efficient only if they are more or less equalized which implies the elimination of decentralization.

Redistribution policies of revenue should be central to be effective. If income distribution aspects of fiscal policy are regionally based, it may result in high-income taxpayers moving out of some regions and low-income taxpayers moving into some jurisdictions and this will defeat the purpose of redistribution. It is obvious that progressive taxes are largely used on the federal government level, while most states and local government taxes tend to be regressive. If this is the case, fiscal decentralization means a shift in the overall tax structure towards a less progressive system. This is precisely why Reagan proposed the New Federalism. Stubblebine concluded: "A sound fiscal federalism would fund federal programs at the federal level and leave the funding of responses to commonly shared concerns to state and local governments."[19]

FISCAL POLICY

The New Federalism and Federal Budget

The central focus in the Reagan strategy to return authority and revenue to state and local governments was to reduce the size of the federal government by reducing the influence of the federal government in the federal system. Reagan administration cut and reversed the dominance of federal aid and federal influence in state and local governments. Reagan drastically reduced the role of Washington in domestic governmental activities. In the assessment of Reagan's fiscal and political strategy, Hugh Hector and Rudolph E. Penner wrote, "Within the conservative movement, two concerns, each identifying something real, had become inextricably linked: the problem of a malfunctioning economy and the problem of a malfunctioning big government. It was an act of political theory to link the latter as the chief cause of the former."[20]

The Reagan administration's policy was based on constant struggle to shift the priorities of the federal government. While Reagan increased defense spending, he cut the federal role in domestic spending. David Stockman, whose budgetary brilliance and indefatigable energy were invaluable to the Reagan administration's early budget cutting success, was obsessively focused on cutting, cutting, and cutting. David Stockman was so fanatically committed to cutting the federal budget that for him, no domestic program was safe. David Stockman was the prototypical supply-sider.[21]

The federal government's budget process was used to reorient public policy. The budget process was also used to shift some responsibility to state and local governments, thereby reducing the federal payment of administrative costs of intergovernmental programs. This meant reduced federal collection and dissemination of information and reduced federal government micromanagement of grant, subsidy, loan and loan guarantee, contract, regulatory, credit, and other government programs contracted to private agencies. Supply-side budgeting differs from the demand-side budgeting. In the past, based on demand-side budgeting, the OMB aggregated the budget requests from federal agencies and reviewed these budget requests based on the administration's projections and the president's priorities. They would increase some items and reduce some, then combine the whole requests to produce a proposed budget that would be sent to Congress. These budget proposals reflected the expression of the fundamental political relationships among agencies, interest groups, and various committees.

With David Stockman as the head of OMB under Reagan, the budget process became an expression of President Reagan's ideological and political agenda. The Reagan administration formulated its budget policy with little or no regard for congressional or interest group opposition. The Reagan budget proposals demonstrated that the administration was determined to challenge Congress and its business as usual approach to the budgeting process. Often Congress refused to accept the budget as a whole, but that did not stop the administration from pursuing the same strategy. Negotiations about any budget amendment were more centralized in Reagan's administration than in any other administration. Reagan's ideological and programmatic priorities were strongly expressed in the budget documents. The budget proposals also contained powerful expressions of the administration's priority of shifting responsibility from federal government to state and local governments.[22]

Ronald Reagan's fiscal federalism demonstrated that he was determined to support the cause of cutting the budget and advancing priorities that focused on the ultimate objective of decentralizing government's responsibility. In his 1987 budget address, he said that his budget proposal "contemplates an end to unwarranted federal intrusion into the state and local sphere and restoration of a more balanced, constitutionally appropriate federalism with more clearly defined roles for the various levels of government .... and to have the federal government get out of the business of paying for local sewage treatment systems, local airports, local law enforcement, subsidies to state maritime schools and local coastal management."[23] The new fiscal federalism was a dramatic turn from an eighty-year trend of domestic spending increases in the federal government budget.

Reagan felt that the federal government had gone too far in its fiscal relationship with the state and local governments. As of January 1, 1981, there were 534 federal categorical grant-in-aid programs available to state and local governments and the total expenditure for federal grant-in-aid had risen in fiscal year 1980 to $91.5 billion. As of January 1, 1984, there were 392 federal categorical grant-in-aid programs available to state and local governments. This is a decline by 142 or about 27% since Reagan came to power.[24]

The administration's first budget illustrates Reagan's determination to stop increase in federal government's role in intergovernmental affairs. Murray Weidenbaum, Reagan's first Chairman of the Council of Economic Advisors, said "the administration's budget also reflects a shift in federal priorities to truly national needs. Both national defense and an adequate social safety net for the truly needy are national priorities and federal responsibilities."[25] However, other existing federal programs were not seen by the administration as vital federal government responsibilities. In 1981, Reagan addressed the mayors at the National League of Cities Convention, stating that: "I know that accepting responsibility, especially for cutbacks, is not easy. But this package should be looked at by state and local governments as a great step toward not only getting America moving again, but toward reconstructing the power system which led to the economic stagnation and urban deterioration."[26] The total federal government's spending for 1981 was $657.2 billion, and $91.5 billion was federal aid to state and local governments, which was 14.4% of the 1981 budget expenditures.

The Omnibus Budget Reconciliation Act of 1981 and consequent congressional budget actions resulted in a fiscal year 1982 budget authority reduction of $45.1 billion; causing a total outlay reduction of $44.1 billion from the level they would have reached if Congress had not adopted Reagan's new policies. This reduced the budget authority by 5.7 percent and outlays by 6.0 percent. Excluding defense expenditure increase and interest on the public debt, the cuts were 12.3 percent in budget authority and 9.4 percent in outlays. Of these budget reductions, a substantial amount came in cuts in federal aid to state and local governments. Grant payments funded federally but administered by state and local governments were reduced $16.35 billion, a 23.5 percent reduction in 1981, while federal grants to state and local governments for their operations and capital projects were reduced $19.07 billion, a 37.7 percent reduction in 1981. All federal aid to state and local governments bore 54.6 percent of reductions in the fiscal year 1982 budget authority. On the average, each budget account had its budget authority compared with 1981 policy levels.[27]

President Reagan's first term in the White House was characterized by a dramatic policy change, a significant reduction in growth of the federal government's domestic programs and a general reduction in intergovernmental grants-in-aid. According to Jack Nelson, "In curbing the growth of social programs, Reagan had waged war against a half century of Democratic philosophy, a philosophy often supported by Republicans."[28]

At the end of Ronald Reagan's first year in office, he said, "I believe that we have started government on a different course, different from anything we've done in the last half century and since Roosevelt began with the New Deal, and that is the recognition that there is a limit to government .... and that there has been a distortion of the relationship between the various echelons of government; federal, state, and local."[29]

Although the fiscal year 1982 budget provided a 12 percent reduction in constant dollars in federal intergovernmental aid, it was projected that FY

1983 would show a 0.7 percent increase. Generally, intergovernmental aid was held constant for FY 1983, but increased funding for transportation programs under the new Surface Transportation Assistance Act would increase all federal aid to state and local government to $93.5 billion. The general trend to state and local governments was at a rapid growth until 1978. Between 1978 and 1983, the total federal grants adjusted for inflation declined nearly 25 percent.[30]

After Reagan sent his first 1981 budget proposal to Congress, he said, "We are not cutting the budget simply for the sake of sounder financial management. This is only a first step toward returning power to states and communities, only a first step toward reordering the relationship between citizen and government."[31] However, in contrast to the historic trend for 50 years, President Reagan had made substantial cuts in domestic spending and trimming in the federal government's role in domestic programs. According to David Broder, Reagan's budget policy reflects that reordering of relationships. He states that there is no doubt that Reagan won the first stage in his battle to halt almost 50 years of unbroken growth of Washington's role in federal system.[32]

Reagan's second term in office was a continuation of his battle to drastically reduce federal intergovernmental spending. During the fiscal year of 1985, state and local governments received $24 from Washington for every $100 they raised on their own. This is in contrast to the high of $32 state and local governments received in 1978.[33] The administration's budget continued the dramatic realignment of spending priorities which began in 1981, with less revenue, a substantial shrinking of much of the domestic budget, and continued buildup of military spending. Form FY 1981 to 1987, total federal grants to state and local governments decreased by 33 percent. From FY 1986 to FY 1987 alone, grants-in-aid and excluding payments to individuals, was reduced from $57.8 billion to $50.6 billion.[34]

President Reagan's proposed fiscal year 1987 budget continued the same downward trend. The National Conference of State Legislators and the National Governors' Association similarly observed the proposed FY 1987 budget: "The President proposes to meet the deficit target by continuing his proposal to reorient national priorities. The President's proposal would decrease federal spending by shifting more responsibilities to the state and local sector, to private industry, and to individuals and families."[35]

During the Reagan administration, federal government aid as a percentage of total state-local outlays dropped by 25 percent in 1981 to about 14 percent in 1987. This reverses the long trend in which federal aid grew faster than state and local own sources of revenue. In 1987, state and local government collected over $500 billion from their own sources. John Shannon wrote, this "fend-for-yourself federalism is slowly affecting a sorting out of governments. Federal policymakers are being forced by fiscal and political realities

to allocate an increasing share of their resources for strictly national government programs: defense, social security, Medicare, and interest on a $2.4 tril-
lion debt."[36]

President Reagan's commitment to federalism is not merely a political
rhetoric. His budgets are based on economic theory which provides a powerful rationale for structuring decision mixing and the financing and delivery of
public services, to the maximum extent possible, on a decentralized basis.
This predisposition toward decentralization is rooted in considerations of efficiency, accountability, manageability and equity. Perhaps no tool wielded by
Reagan to achieve his dream of decentralization has proven more effective
than his budget proposals.

Critics charged that President Reagan's federalism rhetoric was just a
smoke-screen for a radical conservative agenda to dismantle all government
programs. They attacked Reagan's budget proposal with great anger. The administration's explanations that they wanted to dissolve responsibility, sort
out function, and decentralize decision-making were rejected out of hand by
critics as disingenuous. They firmly believed that decentralization and retrenchment went hand in hand. Nathan and Doolittle wrote, "The assumption
was that if social program retrenchment occurred at the federal level in combination with dissolution, the states, too, would pull back on social programs.
The service reductions implied by the federal aid cuts would stick and perhaps even be compounded by parallel state and local action."[37]

Tax Reform

Reagan era was a remarkable period in federal tax policy. During the Reagan
administration, about six major tax revisions were enacted. They were: The
Economic Recovery Tax Act of 1981, the Tax Equity and Fiscal Responsibility Act of 1982, the Social Security Amendments of 1983, the Deficit Reduction Act of 1984, the Tax Reform Act of 1986, and the Omnibus Budget Reconciliation Act of 1987. These tax legislations generated an unusual amount
of debate among the public, Congress and the administration. During this
decade, some minor tax revisions were passed and every year several tax
codes were included in the tax laws. Tax revisions were so common that it
was called it the Tax Decade.

Supply-side economics presented the administration with a theoretical base
for cutting taxes drastically. The argument was that cutting tax rates would
consequently raise tax revenues. Well-known economist Arthur Laffer made
the argument famous.[38] He drew a curve, called the Laffer curve, explaining
that beyond a certain point, an increase in tax rates on taxable activities will
discourage such activities, and will lead to decline in revenues. Laffer instructed Jack Kemp on this assumption and they jumped to a conclusion that

this is what the administration needs to generate growth in the economy. This Laffer curve became popular among the conservatives and big business, providing them with the theoretical authority to pursue their objectives. Reagan strongly believed in Laffer curve tax cut theory. He agreed that an increase in the tax rates would destroy the United States' economy and that tax cuts would generate economic growth and balances the budget.

Tax policy is fundamental to the implementation of Reagan administration's social and economic policies. It has a serious impact on social and economic relationships among the minority and poor; it affects the relationship between the public and the government and the federal and state governments. Tax and budget policies are important components of the Reagan administration's fiscal policies. While budgeting exerted a direct impact on the national economy, taxation provided a potent force that affected the priorities of the United States. The Reagan tax policy was driven by the argument to stimulate growth and reduce the federal budget deficit. While tax reduction policies were implemented to stimulate the economy, other policies were implemented to collect sufficient revenues to reduce the federal deficit. The purpose of this section is to review the extent to which the income tax has been utilized by the Reagan administration as a fiscal policy instrument to shape the national economy. This section deems it necessary to review the trends the administration has taken in the enactment of tax legislation that have altered the application of various fundamental principles of the tax laws. This section will focus on the administration's tax policy amendments enacted during Reagan's era that has direct impact on this study. The discussion of the pertinent tax revisions will include the Economic Recovery Tax Act of 1981 (ERTA), the Tax Equity and Fiscal Responsibility Act of 1982 (TEFRA) and the Tax Reform Act of 1986 (TRA).

Economic Recovery Tax Act of 1981 (ERTA)

One of the centerpieces of the Reagan administration's economic plan was tax reform and tax cuts. The Economic Recovery and Tax Act of 1981 (ERTA) contained several important provisions of the tax code. The two most important codes are the three-year across-the-board cut in income tax rates and the accelerated depreciation of capital investment. Congress passed the Economic Recovery Tax Act of 1981, based on the Reagan administration's tax recommendations. The purpose of the legislation was to create economic recovery through fiscal stimulation of the economy. ERTA 1981 provided the greatest tax cut in the history of the United States economy. It was designed to cut tax by about $224.2 billion. Reagan's former Secretary of the Treasury, Donald Reagan, stated in a congressional hearing committee meeting.

It is clear that frequent policy shifts in response to short-term economic changes are not the solution to our problems. Indeed, they have been a major cause of these problems. As a result of such policies, our nation has come to expect more inflation, more stagnation, more government growth, and more directionless economic policy......... An economic policy focusing on fundamental structural reform will restore long-term strength and prosperity. This can be accomplished only through a consistent, stable set of economic policies maintained over a period of years. The President's economic program represents such a set of policies designed to provide a bold new beginning for the American economy.[39]

There are several factors that motivated the Economic Recovery and Tax Act of 1981. First, Reagan was depending on the potential incentive effects of lower taxes. The administration believed that cutting tax rates would increase incentives to work, save, invest and innovate, and that reducing the tax rates would therefore lead to greater output. On the extreme side of the supply-side, some analyst explained that the tax reduction might even finance itself, which meant that no loss in revenue would occur. The argument was that the tax base would increase more than proportionately to offset the rate of tax reduced. Second, the general population considered taxes too high and government spending too large. The Reagan administration argued that the tax cut would encourage the support for budget cuts due to the high rate of the deficit or what was called a starvation theory of public spending.[40]

The Economic Recovery Tax Act of 1981 was designed to reduce individual income tax rates by about 30 percent at 10 percent increments per year and leaving the top marginal rate at 50 percent. This would lower the tax rate from 70 percent to 50 percent over three years, therefore eliminating the differential in top-bracket tax rates between labor earning and individual income. The provision for Accelerated Cost Recovery emphasized standardized, simplified, and faster depreciation of assets. According to the provision, structures were to be written off in ten years, other machinery in five years, and light equipment in three years. This would replace several asset classes and provide rapid tax recovery. Michael Boskin argued, "Despite the econometric evidence that suggests that a rapid increase in investment would increase productivity only gradually, great emphasis was placed on the ability of those so-called supply-side effects to increase output rapidly."[41]

ERTA introduced the concept of rate indexing to the tax code. Tax rates were to be indexed for inflation starting from 1985. This indexing applied to the graduated rate table for individuals, the zero bracket amount and the personal exemptions. As a result, taxpayers would be protected from higher tax rates known as bracket creep. This is caused by the application of progressively higher tax rates to higher incomes resulting from inflation. ERTA 1981 also contained other provisions that were designed for creating extensive business incentives. The most dramatic amendment was involved with the re-writing of the rules governing depreciation. It replaced the prior depreciation system with the accelerated cost recovery system, which is known as ACRS. ACRS was intended to stimulate capital formulation, increase productivity and improve the nation's competitiveness in international trade by providing substantial tax savings for investments in business assets.

Congress accepted the 1981 tax legislation with little amendment. The Democrats designed an alternative to President Reagan's tax plan, and also to his budget plans. The Democrats tied the third year of the tax reduction to achieving spending reduction goals, therefore reducing the possibility of burgeoning deficits. Reagan opposed this idea on grounds that there would be no pressure placed on spending reduction unless the third year of the tax cut was actually passed. By the time Congress passed the bill, they changed the 10 percent year plan to 5 percent, 10 percent, 15 percent and the tax rate was reduced to 50 percent immediately, rather than over three years as proposed by the Democratic-controlled House Ways and Means Committee. The bill was signed in August of 1981 by the president. He made this remarks when he signed the Economic Recovery Tax Act of 1981, stating, "These bills that I'm about to sign represent a turnaround of almost a half a century of a course this country's been on and mark an end to the excessive growth in government bureaucracy, government spending, government taxing."[42]

The tax savings from ERTA were reflected in reduced revenues to the government. ERTA was proposed to reduce federal revenues by over $267 billion by 1986. ERTA caused an alarming growth in the actual federal budget deficit that by 1982; the federal budget was beginning to hemorrhage. The economy experienced a prolonged recession from mid-1981 to late 1982. Gradually, it became clear that large deficits of historical proportion were accruing and would be in the economic picture for a long time. However, the combination of the recession and high rates before tax interest rates resulted in a sharp fall in an already low rate of investment.[43] As a result of these events, Congress passed the Tax Equity and Fiscal Responsibility Act of 1982.

Tax Equity and Fiscal Responsibility Act of 1982 (TEFRA)

The Tax Equity and Fiscal Responsibility Act (TEFRA) were signed into law by the president in September 1982. It increased tax enforcement and eliminated some loopholes. TEFRA did not affect the individual income tax cut passed in 1981 with the indexing to be implemented in 1985 and many of the provisions of the corporate tax policy enacted in ERTA. TEFRA, however, repealed the further acceleration of depreciation scheduled for 1985–86; it took back about 25 percent of the tax cuts under ERTA. By fiscal year 1988, the net impact was a $215 billion tax reduction.[44] TEFRA was developed to raise revenue in order to reduce the huge budget deficit, which resulted from the Reagan administration's continuation of spending and tax policies. The

principal objective of TEFRA was to restore fiscal responsibility to the income tax laws.

According to Frank Slagle, the economic forecasts by the Office of Management and Budget and Congressional Budget Office were showing a high
federal budget deficit. It was clear that in absence of a change in policy, the
budget deficit might reach $182 billion in fiscal year 1983, $216 billion in
1984, and $233 billion in 1985, based on the forecasts. It was also indicated
that by 1985, it would be the largest deficit in peacetime history, about 5.6
percent gross national product. The huge federal deficit, with then current interest rates, was projected to have extremely serious consequences on the
economy. TEFRA provided tax revenue increases that were relatively modest
compared to the tax reduction of 1981 as provided by ERTA. In 1983, it was
$20.9 billion, in 1984 it was $34.2 billion and in 1985 it was $43.9 billion.[45]

Another principal objective of TEFRA was to correct the economic distortions that were created by the taxing system. On one hand, tax reductions
were seen as a way of alleviating economic distortions, on the other hand, the
overly generous tax incentives were seen as creating economic distortions.
For example, the accelerated depreciation and the investment tax credit were
regarded as overly generous because they encouraged businesses to purchase
equipment for tax benefits rather than their economic usefulness. Slagle argued "indeed, the combination of accelerated depreciation and the investment
tax credit provided tax benefits that were more generous than if the taxpayer
merely took an expense deduction for the cost of equipment in the year it was
placed in service."[46]

TEFRA contained several other provisions. The revenue increase was designed to promote tax equity. Tax equity is a widely accepted goal of tax policy. Tax equity is the distribution of the tax burden in accordance with taxpayers' ability to pay. Tax equity is a way of promoting voluntary compliance
through the imposition of a comparable share of the tax burden on taxpayers.
TEFRA was intended to reverse the trend toward less equity by instituting revenue increases through broadly based tax increases, such as increases in marginal individual income tax rates or taxes on energy consumption. TEFRA provided new withholding laws for interest and dividends at the source, which
were patterned after the wage withholding provisions applicable to employees.
As an adjunct to the withholding provision, TEFRA expanded the informa-
tional return provisions, which required all taxpayers to report the interest they
pay to other taxpayers. It required everyone who paid interest up to $10 or
more to other taxpayers to report the interest they paid to the government.

According to Citizens for Tax Justice, business tax expenditure did not
grow dramatically in the early 1980s despite the large tax cuts for investment
in ERTA 1981 because the decrease in investment was due to the 1981–1982
recession. Business tax expenditure increased in 1983 and 1984. Though, cor-

porate tax expenditures did not grow dramatically during the early 1980s, corporate tax avoidance was, however, the driving force behind the tax reform legislation. This was largely due to the effort made by Citizens for Tax Justice, which was able to point out some businesses that were not paying any income taxes because of special tax provisions.[47]

Tax Reform Act of 1986 (TRA)

The main objective of the Tax Reform Act of 1986 was to broaden the tax base and lower tax rates. The Tax Reform Act of 1986 cut back on special tax provisions, thereby, directly reducing many tax expenditures. It also indirectly reduced most tax rates because the value of deductions depends on the tax rate. By 1990, total tax expenditures as a percentage of GDP were 44 percent lower than in 1986.[48] However, the tax expenditures in the individual income tax in 1990 were higher than in any year prior to 1980. TRA 1986 seemed to have broadened the tax base substantially. With regard to the individual income tax, it eliminated only the growth in tax expenditures that had occurred during the first half of the 1980s.

Congressional Research Service produced a report that explained that a reduction of tax expenditures in the individual income tax not only financed lower income tax rates and higher tax thresholds in TRA 1986, but it also made the tax system fairer. Some special tax provisions treated taxpayers on grounds other than ability to pay and violated a tax principle known as horizontal equity, which means that people in equal circumstances should be treated equally under the tax law. Previously, the code had granted many deductions and credits that were not uniformly utilized by taxpayers with similar income levels. As a result, taxpayers with similar incomes did not necessarily pay a similar amount of tax. In order to increase horizontal equity, it eliminated many of the deductions and credits that were previously permitted. The elimination of many deductions operated to broaden the tax base and simplify the code. Greater horizontal equity was also achieved by placing new restrictions on tax shelters that were previously used by many taxpayers to reduce their tax burdens. Tax fairness also dealt with vertical equity, which means lowest income levels should not have to pay the same rate of tax. The increase in the standard deduction and personal exemptions had the effect of dropping those individuals with the lowest incomes off the tax rolls.

The largest tax savings was realized at the highest and lowest income levels; the middle-income level savings were much less. For example, taxpayers with incomes of less than $10,000 were supposed to have their income liability reduced by about 65.1% and a tax saving of $39. Taxpayers with incomes of $200,000 and above were to get a decrease in income tax liability of 2.4% in 1988 and a tax savings of $3,362. The smallest tax savings, as both a percentage and dollar amount, were at income levels of $50,000 to $100,000. For 1988, the savings were expected to be 1.8% ($150) for tax-payers with incomes between $50,000 and $75,000 and 1.2% ($176) for tax-payers with incomes between $75,000 and $100,000.[49] The tax rate reductions were designed to improve economic efficiency by lowering the marginal tax rates, thereby encouraging work and saving by giving more money in form of wage and investment income to the taxpayers. Further, lower tax rates reduced the value of tax deductions, allowing investment and consumption decisions to be made less on the value of the tax benefits but more on the basis of their economic merits.

NOTES

1. Robert E. Kelleher, "The Theoretical Basis and Historical Origins of Supply-Side Economics," in *Supply-Side Economics: Pro and Con.* eds. G. Thomas Sav and Paul E. Masters (Carrolton, Georgia: West Georgia College, 1982), 15.

2. Kelleher, "The Theoretical Basis and Historical Origins of Supply-Side Economics," 17.

3. Thomas Sowell, "Adam Smith in Theory and Practice," in *Adam Smith and Modern Political Economy,* ed. Gerald P. O'Driscoll (Ames: Iowa State University Press, 1979), 5.

4. Adam Smith, *An Inquiry into the Nature and Cause of the Wealth of Nations,* ed. Edwin Canaan (Chicago: University of Chicago, 1976).

5. Adam Smith, *The Wealth of Nations* (New York: Random House, 1937), 832–833.

6. Jean Baptiste Say, "A Treatise on Political Economy," in *The Critics of Keynesian Economics,* ed. Henry Hazlitt (Princeton, N.J.: Van Nostrand, 1960), 20–21.

7. John Stuart Mill, "Essays on Some Unsettled Questions of Political Economy," in *Critics,* ed. Henry Hazlitt, 26.

8. John Maynard Keynes, *The General Theory of Employment, Interest and Money* (New York: Harcourt, Brace & Co., 1936), 18–26.

9. Thomas J. Hailstones, *A Guide to Supply-Side Economics* (Reston, VA: Reston Publishing Co., 1982), 19.

10. Hailstones, A Guide to Supply-Side Economics, 20.

11. James R. Barth and Joseph J. Cordes, "Supply-Side Economics: Political Claims vs. Economic Reality," in *Supply-Side Economics,* eds. Thomas Sav and Paul Masters, 28.

12. Ronald Reagan, Acceptance Speech, Republican National Convention, Detroit, Michigan, July 17, 1980.

13. W. Craig Stubblebine, "The Economics of the New Federalism," in *Reaganomics: Mid-term Report,* eds. W. Craig Stubblebine and Thomas D. Willett (San Francisco: ICS Press, 1983), 143.

14. "Reagan's Idea of Federalism Called 'Dead'," *The New York Times* 13 December 1982, B17.

15. Advisory Commission on Intergovernmental Relations, *Significant Features of Fiscal Federalism* (Washington, D.C.: Advisory Commission on Intergovernmental Relations, 1995), 3.

16. W. Graig Stubblebine, "The Economics of the New Federalism," in *Reaganomics: Midterm Report,* eds. W. Craig Stubblebine and Thomas D. Willett (San Francisco: ICS Press, 1983), 146–147.

17. Richard A. Musgrave, "The Reagan Administration's Fiscal Policy," in *Reaganomics*, eds. W. Craig Stubblebine and Thomas D. Willet, 129.

18. W. Graig Stubblebine, "The Economics of the New Federalism," in *Reaganomics: Midterm Report*, eds. W. Craig Stubblebine and Thomas D. Willett (San Francisco: ICS Press, 1983), 148.

19. Subblebine, "The Economics of New Federaism," 151.

20. Hugh Hector and Rudolph G. Penner, "Fiscal and Political Strategy in the Reagan Administration," in *The Reagan Presidency: An Early Assessment*, ed. Fred I. Greenstein (Baltimore: The Johns Hopkins University Press, 1983), 28.

21. Jonathan Rauch, "Stockman's Quiet Revolution of OMB May Leave Indelible Mark on Agency," *National Journal* 25 May 1985, 1212–1217.

22. James Carroll and others, "Supply-Side Management in the Reagan Administration," 808.

23. Ronald Reagan's Budget Message of the President, February 5, 1986, *The United States Budget in Brief: Fiscal Year 1987,* 8.

24. Advisory Commission on Intergovernmental Relations, A Catalog of Federal Grant-In-Aid Programs to State and Local Government: Grants Funded FY 1984, December 1984, 1.

25. Murray Weidenbaum, "Strengthening Our Federal System," in *American Federalism: A New Partnership for the Republic,* ed. Robert Hawkins (San Francisco: Institute for Contemporary Studies, 1982), 89–93.

26. Ronald Reagan, Remarks to the National League of Cities, Washington, D.C., March 2, 1981, 1.

27. ohn Ellwood, "Controlling the Growth of Federal Domestic Spending," in *Reductions in U.S.* Domestic Spending, ed. John Ellwood (New Brunswick, N.J.: Transaction Books, 1982), 7–39.

28. Jack Nelson, "The Reagan Legacy," in *Beyond Reagan: The Politics of Upheaval*, ed. Paul Duke (New York: Warner Books, 1986), 83.

29. Nelson, "The Reagan Legacy," 107.

30. Richard P. Nathan and others., *The Consequence of Cuts: The Effects of the Reagan Domestic Program on State and Local Governments* (Princeton, N.J.: Princeton Urban and Regional Research Center, 1983).

31. President Ronald Reagan, Remarks to the Conservative Political Action Committee Conference, Washington, D.C., March 20, 1981.

32. David Broder, "States Learn to Live with End of New Deal," *The Des Moines Register*, 30 November 1983, 9A.

33. Advisory Commission on Intergovernmental Relations, *Significant Features of Fiscal Federalism: 1985–1986 Edition* (Washington, D.C., February 1986) p. 3.

34. United States Conference of Mayors, *The Federal Budget and the Cities: A Review of the President's Budget for Fiscal Year 1987* (Washington, D.C., February, 1986), iii.

35. National Conference of State Legislatures and National Governors' Association, *Impact on the States: The President's 1987 Budget* (Washington, D.C., February, 1986), 1.

36. John Shannon, "The Return to Fend-For-Yourself Federalism: The Reagan Mark," *Intergovernmental Perspective* 13, no. 3/4 (Summer/Fall 1987): 34–36.

37. Richard P. Nathan and others, *Reagan and the States* (Princeton, NJ: Princeton University Press, 1987), 7.

38. Arthur B. Laffer and others, *Foundations of Supply-Side Economics*.

39. Congress, Committee on the Budget, *President Reagan's Economic Program: Hearing before the Committee on the Budget* 97th Cong., 1st. Session, 123, 124, 1981.

40. Michael J. Boskin, *Reagan and the Economy: The Success, Failures, and Unfinished Agenda* (San Francisco: Institute for Contemporary Studies, 1984), 58.

41. Boskin, *Reagan and the Economy*, 59

42. Ronald Reagan, *Public Papers of the Presidents* (Washington, D.C. GPO, 1981), 706.

43. Boskin, *Reagan and the Economy*, 65.

44. Boskin, *Reagan and the Economy*, 66.

45. Frank J. Slagle, "A Decade of Tax Policy: A Reflection of the Economic Dilemmas and Budget Deficit during the 1980s," *New England Law Review*, (Fall 1990) 54.

46. Slagle, A Decade of Tax Policy, 55.

47. Citizens for Tax Justice, *Corporate Income Taxes in the Reagan Years* Oct. 1984, 52.

48. Congressional Budget Office, *The Effects of Tax Reform on Tax Expenditures*, March 1988, 54.

49. Slagle, *A Decade of Tax Policy*, 73.

Chapter Five

Unemployment Among
African Americans

Given the disproportionately large dependency of African Americans on government programs, African Americans have a lot at stake in the politics and economics of government budgets and taxes. Most African Americans depend on a variety of income transfer programs, education, and health-oriented programs. The federal government has used fiscal policy to enhance or slow down economic well being of African Americans.

The Reagan years began with the greatest recession since the Great Depression and concluded with the largest peacetime recovery. The administration drastically curtailed government involvement in promoting domestic policy and enacted a large tax decrease and the biggest defense spending increase. The unprecedented high budget deficits and balance of payments changed the American economy from the world's largest debtor nation to a creditor nation. The United States' economy was transformed from an industrial goods-producing nation to a service providing economy. Several fundamental changes took place in the nation, the number of single parents and unmarried households rose to high proportions, and women assumed more roles in the American economy. The drug problem reached an astronomical height. The beginning of the 1990s brought a geopolitical structural transformation, freedom and democracy in the Soviet Union and the end of the Cold War.

However, the 1980s was an eventful decade and many changes took place in the world political and economic arenas, the effort by African Americans to gain economic equality was impeded by the Reagan administration's fiscal policy. The Reagan era heralded a new theme in which the individual achievement of African Americans became the main strategy for the administration to promote economic equality. Reagan's public policy, which was rooted in a strong conservative political ideology, was based on freedom, personal responsibility, self-help, and laissez-faire. These new watchwords became the strategy for promoting economic equality among African Americans. Obviously, this conservative political rhetoric failed the African Americans as a group. The Reagan era will always be judged by social scientists as a period when the economic progress of African Americans was stalled. Although there are some differences in trends based on class and region, some groups even gain. However, the overall degree of economic inequality in the United States economy in the 1980s was very high.

The main focus of this chapter is to present the facts on the level of unemployment among African Americans during the Reagan era. The chapter presents data to support the statement and the figures will paint a clear picture of a persisting high unemployment rate among African Americans. The racial gap was high and in some regions was very high. The evidence supports the fact that the Reagan administration did little, or did not attempt to address the unemployment problems of African Americans.

FISCAL POLICY IMPLICATIONS FOR AFRICAN AMERICANS

In 1989, the Congressional Black Caucus assessed the performance of the national economy in the decade of the 1980s, and concludes, "A nation's values and concerns for social and economic justice are measured by the fiscal priorities established in its national budget. Judged by these criteria, both the Executive Branch and a majority of the United States Congress failed the moral test of government in the decade of the 1980s."[1]

It is essential to examine the relationship between the Reagan administration's fiscal policy and the high level of unemployment among African Americans. Budget and tax policies, which are the public financial transactions of government, determine the economic well-being of African Americans. The American economic system is designed in such a way that various groups are in constant competition with each other for public goods. Hence, whether the resource is jobs, housing, transportation, health care, elderly care or child care, it is necessary for African Americans to understand and get involved in the fiscal policy process. Thus, we mean fiscal policy as it relates to the budget cycle, taxes, charges and fees, administration of the government debt, bonds, and procurement policy, public corporation and public trust funds

The federal government's fiscal policy is a combination of past, present, and future policy practices and issues. The amount of money allocated for present programs is often determined by the amount of money allocated during the past fiscal year or what is called incremental budgeting. The federal government from time to time chooses one fiscal policy technique over another technique to intervene in domestic public policy issues such as the unemployment problem. Thus, the economic well-being of African Americans depends on the form of fiscal policy chosen by the federal government, regardless of whether African Americans are directly or indirectly the target of the fiscal policy. Fiscal decision-making is a very complicated task that involves various economic equity and equality issues, and the financial and accounting complexity, which characterizes the budget and tax policy.

However, there are some basic facts we need to note about the relationship between fiscal policies and African American political and economic aspirations. African Americans are disproportionately dependent upon government funds in order to advance their economic and political equality. African Americans are yet to consolidate their own financial groups to gain control over the macroeconomic, institutional, and household dependencies. The stability of these levels of dependencies was shaken by the Reagan administration fiscal policy—the new emphasis on individual freedom, pay for yourself and pay as you go conservative ideology. The administration's tax and expenditure approach, deficits, balance of trade and balance of payment deficits, and Reagan's conservative political ideology led to a new emphasis in fiscal decision-making. In the era of hostile tax policy and budget reduction, African Americans are still heavily dependent on federal, state, and local governments for most of their institutional and household funding and are consequently subjected to most of the hostile budget and tax policies.

Gramm-Rudman-Hollings Balanced Budget and Emergency Deficit Control Act of 1985 and the Tax Reform Act of 1986, and various states and local governments' fiscal responses to the federal government fiscal policy are threatening the African American economic and political gains from the civil rights movement of the 1960s era. African Americans are actively trying to change the national, state and local fiscal priorities through lobbying, the courts and mass media exposure of federal government budget and tax priorities. African Americans support the fiscal philosophy that emphasizes a political economy of fiscal policy on econometrics of resource distribution and redistribution, and it is also an issue of morally correct fiscal decisions made by the government. The concern of this chapter is whether the fiscal policy of the Reagan administration empowered or helped the African Americans, particularly those with pressing needs, to improve their unemployment situation.

REAGAN'S NEW ETHICS OF FISCAL CONTROL AND FISCAL SUPPORT

Reagan's rise to power in 1980 signified a drastic change from federal government responsiveness policy on social issues of the 1960s and 1970s. Before

Ronald Reagan, government responsiveness accelerated the transition of
African Americans to a higher economic and political self-determination.[2] The
Reagan administration radically reduced government expenditure in many social support programs and transferred some of those responsibilities to states
and local government. The president's fiscal strategy was to cut domestic
spending and taxes, and increase defense spending. Lenneal Henderson explains:

> The ethical thrust resulting from most of these retrenchment initiatives was that
> government's fiscal burdens had become too heavy, that the beleaguered Amer-
> ican taxpayer should not be expected to bear the cost of social change, and that
> citizens should become more vigilant about fiscal decision-making. Implicit in
> this thrust was a rejection of social transformation ideology apparent in the
> 1960s. Neither an ethic of governmental responsiveness to the expensive needs
> of the impoverished nor a tolerance for the time and cost required for respon-
> siveness to result in social transformation was evident in this ethic.[3]

Reagan new fiscal ethic had a serious impact on African Americans and the
politically weak. The administration ethic was based on conservative political ideology with profound implications.

Gramm-Rudman-Hollings (GRH) or the Balanced Budget and Emergency
Deficit Control Act of 1985 and the Tax Reform Act of 1986 represent the
Reagan administration's obsession with the politics and economics of fiscal
control. These impulsive fiscal control tendencies resulted from frustration
with the inability to effectively reduce the federal government deficit. During
the Reagan era, every public policy proposal, regardless of its inherent value
or ethical imperative, was subjected to the deficit reduction test. The federal
deficit grew from $60 billion in 1980 to $220.5 billion in 1985, increasing
from 2.3 to 5.3 percent of the gross national product (GNP) of the U.S. In
1985, the administration maintained a high priority on deficit reduction because they were concerned about the economic and political implications of
a high deficit; concerned about the failure of the National Economic Recovery Tax Act of 1981 and other policy measures designed to stimulate economic growth, and about the impact of the failures of these policy initiatives
on the upcoming 1986 and 1988 elections.

Under the Gramm-Rudman-Hollings Act, sequestration-triggering decisions were the functions of the Congressional Budget Office (CBO), the Office of Management and Budget (OMB) and the General Accounting Office
(GAO). CBO and OMB were to estimate jointly the size of the deficit for the
next fiscal year and to determine if the deficit exceeded the specified limit by
more than $10 billion. GRH set various deficit reduction targets, and the Act
eliminated the congressional budgetary role. In July 1986, the Supreme

Court, in the case of Bowsher v. Syner, ruled against the automatic sequestration provision that required the Controller General and the head of GAO to perform an executive function assigned by the Constitution to the Congress. However, GRH had a provision for presidential sequestration on enactment of a joint resolution. This procedure was not automatic, but it was constitutional.

This significant event allowed African Americans to follow the congressional debate in Senate and House committees. With the shift in role, African Americans can track the analyses and proposals of the CBO that are most likely to influence congressional decisions.

The CBO expert analyses and proposals were very critical for groups supporting an increase in social programs for the needy. CBO also monitored the congressional ethical debate in key Senate and House committees on spending priorities. As a result of the elimination of the GAO role by the Supreme Court's decision, the direct conflicts between Congress and the president became more intense. Who will win in such a struggle, the Congress or the President, depends on the strategies used by the opponents and the influence of various interest groups that the prevailing party was willing to take into consideration. However, the Congress or the president did not take any deficit policy position that would have taken the federal budget deeply into social intervention or that sustains all discretionary social programming at current funding levels plus inflation. Except in some instances, the roles of responsive fiscal policies for African Americans shifted to the state and local governmental levels.

Gramm-Rudman-Hollings Act was the major legislative initiative for deficit reduction, and the Tax Reform Act of 1986 (TRA) was the leading legislative action on federal government revenue. The main policy objective of TRA included fairness; revenue growth simplification of tax regulations and forms; a separate standard reduction for households headed by a single parent; the removal of more than six million poor households from the tax pools; low-income housing depreciation; continued deductibility of state and local income taxes; and retroactive repeal of the investment tax credit. The decline in the amount of various income transfer programs contributed to the high level of unemployment, labor market problems and poverty among African Americans. Darity and Myers agree:

> Blacks unequivocally rely in disproportionate numbers on such programs for income. One-quarter of all blacks are enrolled in the Medicaid program, one quarter receives food stamps, 20 percent receive support form the AFDC program, and one in seven blacks lives in federally subsidized housing. One quarter of black households with school children five to 18 years old receives free or reduced-price school lunches.[4]

Income losses due to unemployment in many African American households mean a substantial reduction in federal, state, and local government revenue. Consequently, the revenue losses translate into little or no policy to address African American unemployment issues as seen in President Ronald Reagan's fiscal policy. The psychological and administrative problems created between taxpayer and the complex tax provisions of the Tax Reform Act of 1986 intensified.

It is also vital to understand the intergovernmental ramification of Reagan's fiscal policy and their impact on African Americans. Immediately after the enactment of the Tax Reform Act, Tax Conformity became an issue. Tax Conformity is the extent to which state and local government's income tax law conforms to federal government tax policy. Some states that attempted to change the tax laws according to the federal tax policy, realized a revenue windfall at the expense of state taxpayers and the needy in particular. The states that embraced a more gradualist approach displayed sensitivity to voter intolerance of higher state taxes exhibited in most of the tax reform of the 1980s. Budget wise, the elimination of state and local revenue sharing funds and the reductions in most categories of block grant funding distributed from federal to state and local governments were both economically and politically expensive for African Americans. There was an increase in demand for social services in states and local governments where African American populations were high.

AFRICAN AMERICAN UNEMPLOYMENT RATES

In the 1980s African Americans were still more than twice as likely as whites to be unemployed. In 1993 the unemployment rate for African American workers was 12.9 percent, compared to 6.0 percent for whites. The unemployment rate for Hispanics was 10.6 percent. Over the past decade, their labor force swelled by nearly 50 percent. While some indicators show that Hispanic workers tend to be somewhat more successful in the labor market than African Americans, they still lag behind white workers in most labor market performance categories (see Table 5.1). The higher unemployment rates for African American workers occur across all major age-sex groups. In 1993 the rates for African American adult men and women were 12.1 and 10.6 percent, respectively, compared to 9.4 and 9.8 percent for Hispanics and 5.6 and 5.1 percent for whites. African American teenagers, a group especially vulnerable to joblessness, had an unemployment rate of 38.9 percent in 1993, compared with 26.2 percent for Hispanic teens and 16.2 percent for white teenagers (Table 5.1).

Blacks and Hispanics to lagged considerably behind whites according to nearly every measure of labor market success. Blacks comprised the

Table 5.1. Employment Status of Major Age-Sex Groups by Race and Hispanic Origin, 1983 and 1993 Annual Averages

Employment status, sex and age	*(Numbers in thousands)*					
	Black		Hispanic Origin		White	
TOTAL	1983	1993	1983	1993	1983	1993
Civilian noninstitutional population	18,925	22,329	11,029	15,753	150,805	163,921
Civilian labor force	11,647	13,943	7,033	10,377	97,021	109,359
Percent of population	61.5	62.4	63.8	65.9	64.3	66.7
Employed	9,375	12,146	6,072	9,272	88,893	102,812
Percent of population	49.5	54.4	55.1	58.9	58.9	62.7
Unemployed	2,272	1,796	961	1,104	8,128	6,547
Unemployment rate	19.5	12.9	13.7	10.6	8.4	6.0
Men, 20 years and over						
Civilian noninstitutional population	7,360	9,031	4,771	7,063	65,581	73,711
Civilian labor force	5,533	6,498	4,014	5,871	51,716	57,115
Percent of population	75.2	72.0	84.1	83.1	78.9	7.5
Employed	4,531	5,710	3,523	5,318	47,618	53,897
Percent of population	61.6	63.2	73.8	75.3	72.6	73.1
Unemployed	1,002	789	491	553	4,098	3,218
Unemployment rate	18.1	12.1	12.2	9.4	7.9	5.6
Women, 20 years and over						
Civilian noninstitutional population	9,340	11,200	4,954	7,176	72,601	79,631
Civilian labor force	5,306	6,668	2,429	3,846	38,119	46,413
Percent of population	56.8	59.5	49.0	53.6	52.5	58.3
mployed	4,428	5,962	2,127	3,467	35,476	44,028
Percent of population	47.4	53.2	42.9	48.3	48.9	55.3
Unemployed	878	706	302	378	2,643	2,385
Unemployment rate	16.5	10.6	12.4	9.8	6.9	5.1
Both sexes, 16 to 19 years						
Civilian noninstitutional population	2,225	2,099	1,304	1,515	12,623	10,579
Civilian labor force	809	776	590	660	7,186	5,381
Percent of population	36.4	37.0	45.3	43.6	56.9	55.1
Employed	416	474	423	487	5,799	4,887
Percent of population	18.7	22.6	32.4	32.2	45.9	46.2
Unemployed	392	302	167	173	1,387	943
Unemployment rate	48.5	38.9	28.4	26.2	19.3	16.2

Source: US. Department of Labor, Bureau of Labor Statistics.

largest minority group in the United States—over 22 million persons of working age (16 years and over) in 1993, of whom 13.9 million were in the labor force. Blacks held proportionately fewer jobs than whites and had much higher rates of unemployment. This problem was compounded by the fact that, once unemployed, blacks tend to remain jobless longer than whites. Among those who are employed, blacks were much more likely than whites to be working part-time involuntarily and to held lower-skilled, lower-paying jobs. Blacks also comprised a disproportionately large number of discouraged workers—persons outside the labor force who want a job, but gave up looking for work because they believe their job search would be in vain.[5]

The higher unemployment rates for African Americans mean that they spend more time than whites looking for jobs. In 1993, the average duration of unemployment for African American workers was 19.3 weeks, compared to 17.7 weeks for whites. Surprisingly, the average duration for Hispanic workers tends to be somewhat lower than for whites at 16.5. This was due to the fact that there was a higher concentration of Hispanics in occupations where the duration of unemployment tends to be relatively short. African Americans are more likely than whites to be reported as discouraged workers—persons who indicate that they want a job but are not looking for work because they believe their efforts would be in vain, and hence are not classified as unemployed. The existence of a sizable number of people who do not participate in the job market because of their discouragement over job prospects is a serious labor market problem, since these people represent additional labor resources that are not being utilized. African American workers are also more likely than whites to have to settle for part-time work even though they would have preferred full-time employment. For both African Americans and Hispanics, about 1 in 10 workers were employed part time for economic reasons in 1993, compared to 1 in 20 white workers.

African Americans hold proportionately fewer jobs than whites. The percent of the African American working-age population that was employed (the employment-population ratio) was 54.4 percent in 1993, compared to 58.9 percent for Hispanics and 62.7 percent of whites. Although there has been occupational upgrading among African Americans over the past decade, they have continued to be concentrated in less-skilled, lower-paying occupations. In 1993, African American men were about half as likely as white men to be employed as managers or professionals, and much more likely to be employed as operators, fabricators, and laborers. African American women were much more likely than white women to be employed in lower-paying service occupations (see Table 5.2).

Table 5.2. Employed Persons by Occupation, Sex, Race and Hispanic Origin 1993 Annual Averages

(Percent distribution)

Occupation	Men			Women		
	Black	Hispanic Origin	White	Black	Hispanic Origin	White
Total employed (thousands)	5,957	5,603	56,397	6,189	3,669	46,415
Percent	100.0	100.0	100.0	100.0	100.0	100.0
Managerial and professional specialty	14.7	12.4	27.1	20.5	16.6	29.3
Executive, administrative, and managerial	7.7	7.2	14.5	5.1	7.9	12.3
Professional specialty	6.9	5.2	12.6	12.4	8.7	17.0
Technical, sales, and administrative support	18.1	15.5	20.8	37.8	39.2	43.9
Technicians and related support	2.7	1.8	3.1	3.6	2.7	3.7
Sales occupations	6.5	7.4	12.0	9.1	11.5	13.0
Administrative support, including clerical	8.9	6.3	5.7	25.1	25.0	27.2
Service occupations	19.4	16.2	9.2	27.5	25.6	16.7
Private household	.1	.1	.1	2.4	5.2	1.5
Protective service	4.9	2.2	2.6	1.3	.5	.6
Service, except private household and protective	14.4	13.9	6.6	23.8	19.9	14.7
Precision production, craft and repair	14.0	20.0	19.6	2.5	2.8	2.0
Mechanics and repairers	5.1	6.0	6.8	.3	.2	.3
Construction trades	5.3	8.4	8.0	.2	.1	.2
Other precision production, craft, and repair	3.6	5.6	4.8	2.0	2.5	1.5
Operators, fabricators, and laborers	30.6	27.4	18.9	11.5	14.0	7.0
Machine operators, assemblers, and inspectors	9.6	11.0	6.7	8.4	11.1	4.7
Transportation and material moving occupations	10.6	7.3	6.7	1.1	.6	.8
Handlers, equipment cleaners, helpers, and laborers	10.4	9.1	5.4	2.0	2.3	1.5
Farming, forestry, and fishing	3.2	8.4	4.5	.3	1.7	1.0

Note: Detail may not add to 100.0 percent because of rounding.
Source: U.S. Department of Labor. Bureau of Labor Statistics.

PRE-REAGAN, REAGAN, AND POST-REAGAN
(BUSH) PERIODS OF NATIONAL EMPLOYMENT AND
UNEMPLOYMENT LEVELS FOR AFRICAN AMERICANS

The entire period of Reagan years represented a roller-coaster ride for employment rates for African Americans. The employment rate for all African American groups generally declined from 1980 through 1983. The same situation was also true for whites. Between 1988 and 1989, the employment rate slightly increased. However, the African American employment rate experienced a historical decline during the Reagan era. During the pre-Reagan period, the average employment population for African American men was 69.2 percent compared to the Reagan, and Bush periods' average of 64.6 percent, a difference of 4.6 percentage points.[6] White male average fell from 77.1 percent to 74.2 percent. Hence, relative inequality increased for males as the Black and White index (B/W index) declined, from an average value of 90 percent in the pre-Reagan period to 87 percent during the Reagan and post-Reagan periods. African American women had a higher average employment population ratio than white women. The ratio from African American women was 47.4 percent, compared to 43.9 percent for white women. The B/W index was 1.08 in the pre-Reagan years and during the Reagan and post-Reagan era, it fell to 0.99 (See Table 5.3).

During the post-Reagan era, the employment rates for the total African American population continued to decline from 1989 through 1992; the employment rate for African American men declined slightly each year after 1988. Inequality also worsened slightly during 1992 for the total African American population. African American inequality as measured by the B/W index had worsened for five consecutive years. For the first nine months of 1992, African American males 20 years and over were only 86.7 percent as likely to be employed as white men. The gap in the African American male's adult employment rate in 1992 cost African American males about 864,000 jobs. African American women were 96.7 percent as likely as white women to be employed during the same period. The difference in employment rates translated into about 199,000 jobs for African American adults. African American teenagers had an employment ratio of only 23.0 percent compared to 45.2 percent for white teenagers. The difference in jobs translates into a shortfall of about 461,000. For the total African American population, the aggregate job shortfall was about 1,564,000 jobs (See Table 5.3).

A perusal of the data in Table 5.4 shows that unemployment rates rose sharply for African Americans during 1992. The 1992 unemployment rate rose from 12.4 percent in 1991 to 14.6 percent in 1992 for the total African

Table 5.3. Civilian Employment—Population Ratio by Race, Sex, and Age: Selected Years

	Total Population			Men (20 years +)			Women (20 years +)			Both sexes (16–19 years)		
	Black	White	B/W	Black	White	B/W	Black	White	B/W	Black	White	B/W
*1992	54.5	62.4	0.873	63.2	72.9	0.867	53.2	55.0	0.967	23.0	45.2	0.509
1991	55.1	62.6	0.880	64.9	73.4	0.884	53.5	54.8	0.976	22.9	46.6	0.491
1990	56.2	63.6	0.884	66.1	75.0	0.881	54.2	55.3	0.980	26.6	49.8	0.534
1989	56.8	63.8	0.890	66.9	75.4	0.887	54.6	54.9	0.995	28.8	51.5	0.559
1988	56.3	63.1	0.892	67.0	75.1	0.892	53.9	54.0	0.995	27.5	51.0	0.539
1987	55.6	62.3	0.892	66.4	74.7	0.890	53.0	53.8	0.987	27.1	49.4	0.549
1986	54.1	61.5	0.879	65.1	74.3	0.887	51.6	52.0	0.992	25.1	48.8	0.514
1985	53.4	61.0	0.876	64.6	74.3	0.869	50.9	51.0	0.999	24.6	48.5	0.508
1984	52.3	60.5	0.865	64.1	74.3	0.863	49.8	50.2	0.992	21.9	48.0	0.457
1983	49.5	58.9	0.840	61.6	72.6	0.848	47.4	48.9	0.970	18.7	45.9	0.407
1982	49.4	58.8	0.840	61.4	73.0	0.841	47.5	48.4	0.981	19.0	45.9	0.415
1981	51.3	60.1	0.854	64.3	75.2	0.855	48.5	48.6	0.998	21.9	48.8	0.448
1980	52.2	60.1	0.868	65.6	75.7	0.867	49.1	47.9	1.024	23.9	50.8	0.468
1979	53.8	60.7	0.886	69.0	77.4	0.892	49.4	47.4	1.041	25.3	52.7	0.481
1978	53.6	60.0	0.893	69.1	77.2	0.895	49.3	46.1	1.069	25.2	52.4	0.491
1977	51.4	58.7	0.876	67.4	74.8	0.9(1	46.9	44.4	1.056	22.2	50.2	0.442
1976	50.8	57.6	0.882	66.7	76.0	0.877	46.3	43.1	1.075	22.3	47.9	0.466
1975	50.1	56.6	0.885	66.4	75.8	0.877	44.8	41.9	1.069	23.1	46.6	0.495
1974	53.5	58.3	0.918	71.8	78.6	0.914	46.9	42.2	1.112	25.9	49.3	0.524
1973	54.5	59.2	0.936	73.6	79.2	0.930	47.2	41.6	1.134	27.3	49.0	0.557
1972	53.7	57.4	0.936	73.0	79.0	NA	46.5	40.6	1.145	25.2	46.4	0.543

*Average of the first three quarters of 1992
Source: U.S. Department of Labor, Bureau of Labor Statistics, Handbook of Labor Statistics, June 1985, and Employment and Earnings, January 1992 and October 1992.

American population. Unemployment was up almost 2 percentage points for African American men, rising from 11.7 percent in 1991 to 13.6 percent in 1992. For African American women, the increase was to 11.6 percent, up from 10.2 percent; the teenage unemployment rate rose from 36.2 percent to 39.8 percent. Although white employment rate rose also, African American unemployment rose faster. The overall B/W index increased to 2.2 from 2.1. The B/W index remained constant for African American women and dropped slightly for black teenagers. The aggregate impact of the differential in unemployment rates during 1992 was to create excess unemployment of 1,059,000 persons, made up of 471,000 men, 415,000 women, and 173,000 teenagers (see Table 5.4).

During the Reagan, and post-Reagan eras, patterns of unemployment reflected the patterns examined for the employment population ratio. Unemployment rates increased sharply for all groups from 1980 through 1983. Then the unemployment rate experienced a roller-coaster ride through 1989. African American unemployment rates were higher throughout the Reagan and post-Reagan years than the pre-Reagan years. Throughout the Reagan and post-Reagan years, the unemployment rate for the total African American population averaged 14.5 percent. The lowest rate of unemployment for African Americans during the Reagan and post-Reagan periods was 11.3 percent in 1990. During the pre-Reagan era, African Americans unemployment rate averaged 12.4 percent. All groups experienced increases in the unemployment rate during the Reagan and post-Reagan years. The unemployment rates for African American men averaged 13.0 percent compared to 9.4 percent during the pre-Reagan era. Equally for African American women, the unemployment rate during the Reagan and post-Reagan periods was 12.3 percent compared to 10.6 percent during the pre-Reagan era. African American teenager's unemployment rate was 37.7 percent compared to 36.0 percent during pre- and post-Reagan periods.

The African American unemployment rate was absolutely higher during the Reagan and post-Reagan years, and the inequality in unemployment rates increased. For the total African American population, the average B/W index was 2.36 during Reagan and post-Reagan periods compared to 2.16 in the pre-Reagan era. The differential for African American men averaged 2.2 to 1 in the pre-Reagan and post-Reagan era. The inequality index for African American women rose from 1.92 during pre-Reagan to 2.32 in the Reagan and post-Reagan eras. The ratio of African American teenagers to white teenagers' unemployment averaged 2.27 in the period before Reagan and was 2.47 during Reagan and post-Reagan years. Hence, the racial disparity in unemployment increased for all African Americans (see Table 5.4).

Table 5.4. Unemployment Rates by Race, Sex, and Age: Selected Years

	Total Population			Men (20 years +)			Women (20 years +)			Both sexes (16–19 years)		
	Black	White	B/W	Black	White	B/W	Black	White	B/W	Black	White	B/W
*1992	14.6	6.5	2.2	13.6	6.4	2.1	11.6	5.4	2.1	39.8	17.2	2.3
1991	12.4	6.0	2.1	11.7	5.8	2.0	10.2	4.9	2.1	36.2	14.9	2.4
1990	11.3	4.7	2.4	10.4	4.3	2.4	9.8	4.1	2.4	31.1	13.4	2.3
1989	11.4	4.5	2.5	10.0	3.9	2.6	9.8	4.0	2.5	32.4	12.7	2.6
1988	11.7	4.7	2.5	10.1	4.1	2.5	10.4	4.1	2.5	32.5	13.1	2.5
1987	13.0	5.3	2.5	11.1	4.8	2.3	11.6	4.6	2.5	33.4	13.3	2.5
1986	14.5	6.0	2.4	12.9	5.3	2.4	12.4	5.4	2.3	39.3	15.6	2.5
1985	15.1	6.2	2.4	13.2	5.4	2.4	13.1	5.7	2.3	40.2	15.7	2.6
1984	15.9	6.5	2.4	14.3	5.7	2.5	13.5	5.8	2.3	42.7	16.0	2.7
1983	19.5	8.4	2.3	18.1	7.9	2.3	16.5	6.9	2.4	48.5	19.3	2.5
1982	18.9	8.6	2.2	17.8	7.8	2.3	15.4	7.3	2.1	34.6	14.4	2.4
1981	15.5	6.7	2.3	13.3	5.6	2.4	13.4	5.9	2.3	41.5	17.3	2.4
1980	14.1	6.3	2.2	12.2	5.2	2.3	11.7	5.6	2.1	38.6	15.5	2.5
1979	12.2	5.1	2.4	9.1	3.6	2.5	10.8	5.0	2.2	15.5	17.4	0.9
1978	12.8	5.2	2.5	9.3	3.7	2.5	11.2	5.2	2.2	49.0	20.4	2.4
1977	13.9	6.2	2.2	10.5	4.6	2.3	12.2	6.2	2.0	41.1	15.4	2.7
1976	13.8	7.0	2.0	11.2	5.4	2.1	11.6	6.8	1.7	39.3	16.9	2.3
1975	14.7	7.9	1.9	12.4	6.2	2.0	12.1	7.5	1.6	39.4	17.9	2.2
1974	10.4	5.0	2.1	7.3	3.5	2.1	8.7	5.0	1.7	34.9	14.0	2.5
1973	9.3	4.3	2.2	5.9	2.9	2.0	8.5	4.3	2.0	31.4	12.6	2.5
1972	10.4	5.1	2.0	7.0	3.6	1.9	9.0	4.9	1.8	35.4	14.2	2.5

*Average of the first three quarters of 1992
Source: U.S. Department of Labor, Bureau of Labor Statistics, *Handbook of Labor Statistics*, June 1985, and *Employment and Earnings*, January 1992 and October 1992.

REGIONAL EMPLOYMENT AND UNEMPLOYMENT RATE

The unemployment situation for African Americans continued to worsen until 1992. The African American employment and unemployment conditions differ in regions and places. The tables in this section present the best available data to evaluate the level of unemployment among African Americans in many of the regions and places compared with the national level. Table 5.5 presents the employment population ratios for Northeast, Midwest, and South and West census regions as related to the general ratio. The general ratios declined in each region for the total African American population and in each subgroup in comparison to the 1990 level. In 1991, the African American employment rate for the Midwest was the lowest with only about 49.7 percent of the African American population employed. The highest ratio was in the Western region with 57.6 percent of African Americans employed. The ratio for African Americans in the Northeast was 53.5 percent and the ratio for the South was 56.7 percent.

For African American men, the distribution followed the same pattern as seen in the total African American population. The African American men had their lowest employment rates in the Midwest, which was 55.1 percent, and the highest in the West at 65.3 percent. The employment population rate in the South was 62.4 percent and in the Northeast region the employment rate for African American men was 58.1 percent. As can be seen from the data in Table 5.5, the employment population ratio for women and teenagers followed the same pattern presented for the total population of African Americans. Although, it should be noted that for the African American women, there was a change in positions in the South and West. In other regions, the patterns were the same. African American teenagers in the South experienced the highest employment population ratio. The second highest employment population ratio for African American teenagers was in the West, followed by the Midwest; the Northeast was the region with the lowest employment rate for African American teenagers.

A close look at the Table 5.5 reveals that white employment population rates were higher than African American employment population rates for the total population and for each of the subgroups in all of the regions. Based on the pattern of B/W values, inequality for the total population was the highest in the Midwest where African Americans were only 76.8 percent as likely as white to be employed. The Northeast was the second highest, where African Americans were 87.8 percent as likely as whites to be employed. The West and the South tied for the regions with the lowest inequality in employment rates, with a B/W index of 91.7 each. The order of inequality, from highest to lowest, for men was the Midwest, Northeast, South, and West. The order for

Table 5.5. Employment Population Ratios by Sex and Race by Regions, 1991

	Total Population			Men (20 years +)			Women (20 years +)			Both sexes (16 to 19 years)		
	Black	White	B/W	Black	White	B/W	Black	White	B/W	Black	White	B/W
Northeast	53.5	60.9	97.8	59.1	70.0	83.0	49.8	52.7	94.5	18.1	44.0	41.1
Midwest	49.7	64.7	76.8	55.1	73.1	75.4	45.5	56.9	80.0	21.7	53.1	40.9
South	56.7	61.9	91.7	62.4	71.2	87.6	52.1	53.3	97.7	24.2	44.3	54.6
West	57.6	62.8	91.7	65.3	71.7	91.1	50.5	54.1	93.3	22.8	44.7	51.0

Source: U.S. Department of Labor, Bureau of Labor Statistics, *Geographic Profile of Employment and Unemployment. 1991, August 1992.*

both women and teenagers from most inequality to the least was the Midwest, Northeast, West, and South. In general, inequality as measured by the B/W index, increased in all regions for the total population and for each subgroup since 1990. The Western region was an exception where the B/W measure improved for the total men and women population.

Table 5.6 presents unemployment ratios for the Northeast, Midwest, South, and West census regions for 1991. We should observe that the unemployment rate was uniformly higher for the total African Americans and for all subgroups in each of the regions. For the total African American group, the unemployment rate was highest in the Midwest at 6.3 percent, 12.2 percent in the Northeast, 11.4 percent in the South and 11.1 percent in the West. The unemployment rate for African American men was 17.8 percent, 14.8 percent for African American women, and 42.7 percent for African American teenagers. It is interesting to note that African American men had their lowest unemployment rate in the South, even though it was still high at 11.2 percent. The African American men unemployment rate in the West was 11.4 percent and 14.4 percent in the Northeast. The African American women unemployment rate was lowest in the Northeast at 10.0 percent, and 11.7 percent for the South. The Midwest had the highest unemployment rate for African American women at 14.8 percent. African American teenagers had their lowest unemployment rate in the West at 34.8 percent, 35.6 percent in the Northeast, and highest in the Midwest at 42.7 percent.

Table 5.6 revealed that the greatest inequality existed in the Midwest, where all the African American groups had about three times the unemployment rates of the corresponding white groups. The B/W indexes in the Midwest ranged from 2.964 to 3.020. Inequality was greatest for adults in the Midwest. Adult females experienced more inequality than the adult males. Based on the B/W measurement, the South generally had the next highest level of inequality, with the index ranging from 1.965 for adult males to 2.16 for adult females. In the Northeast, inequality for females was 1.667 and 2.145 for teenagers. The West, in general, had the least inequality with a B/W index of 1.652 for men and 1.767 for females. It should be noted that women experienced the highest levels of inequality in every region except the Northeast region. The relative degree of inequality as measured by the B/W index declined during 1991 for all categories in every region. This decline was caused by the unemployment rate for African Americans rising relatively slower than that for whites. However, in most groups, the absolute increase in the unemployment rate for African Americans was higher in each region.

Table 5.7 displays data on the employment situation in selected large Standard Metropolitan Statistic Areas (MSAs) with a significant number of African Americans. As can be seen from Table 5.7, African American em-

Table 5.6. Unemployment Rates by Regions, 1991

	Total Population			Men (20 years +)			Women (20 years +)			Both sexes (16 to 19 years)		
	Black	*White*	*B/W*	*Black*	*White*	*B/W*	*Black*	*White*	*B/W*	*Black*	*White*	*B/W*
Northeast	12.2	6.7	1.821	14.4	7.3	1.973	10.0	6.0	1.667	35.6	16.6	2.145
Midwest	16.3	5.5	2.964	17.8	6.0	2.967	14.8	4.9	3.020	42.7	14.4	2.965
South	11.4	5.6	2.036	11.2	5.7	1.965	11.7	5.4	2.167	34.8	17.0	2.047
West	11.1	6.5	1.708	11.4	6.9	1.652	10.6	6.0	1.767	29.9	18.0	1.656

Source: U.S. Department of Labor, Bureau of Labor Statistics, *Geographic Profile of Employment and Unemployment. 1991,* August 1992.

96   Chapter Five

Table 5.7.   Employment-to-Population Ratios for Selected SMSAs by Race, 1991

Metro Area	Black Emp/Pop Ratio	White Emp/Pop Ratio	B/W
Hartford, CT	75.8	64.5	1.175
Phoenix, AZ	70.7	64.1	1.103
Seattle, WA	69.7	68.7	1.000
Charlotte, NC	69.0	69.1	0.994
Dallas-Ft. Worth, TX	65.3	72.9	0.896
Kansas City KS	65.2	68.9	0.946
Washington, DC	64.7	72.3	0.895
Fort Lauderdale. FL	64.4	54.1	1.190
Atlanta, GA	63.8	71.3	0.895
Norfolk, VA	63.6	66.7	0.954
Denver-Boulder. CO	63.2	71.6	0.883
Louisville, KY	60.9	64.4	0.946
Houston, TX	60.6	68.4	0.886
Bergen-Passaic, NJ	60.1	61.7	0.974
Newark, NJ	59.4	62.5	0.950
Nassau-Suffolk, NY	59.3	60.9	0.974
Tampa-St. Petersburg, FL	58.9	57.9	1.017
San Antonio, TX	58.2	57.1	1.019
Baltimore, MD	57.7	66.3	0.870
Riverside, CA	57.2	57.6	0.993
Rochester, NY	57.1	66.7	0.856
Minneapolis-St. Paul, MN	56.5	73.8	0.766
Columbus, OH	55.6	67.1	0.829
Memphis, TN	53.7	63.3	0.848
Los Angeles, CA	53.3	61.8	0.862
Cleveland. OH	53.1	59.9	0.886
Miami. FL	52.5	60.7	0.865
Pittsburgh, PA	52.4	55.8	0.939
Dayton, OH	51.9	62.1	0.836
Oakland, CA	51.6	65.3	0.790
Cincinnati, OH	51.5	67.2	0.766
Philadelphia. PA	50.9	62.2	0.818
St. Louis, MO	50.3	53.5	0.797
New York. NY	50.2	53.5	0.938
Indianapolis, IN	49.6	67.3	0.737
Boston, MA	49.3	64.1	0.769
New Orleans, LA	49.0	62.8	0.780
Milwaukee, WI	48.9	69.1	0.708
Providence. RI	46.7	61.5	0.759
Chicago, IL	46.3	66.9	0.692
Oklahoma City, OK	43.8	64.7	0.677
Detroit, MI	42.6	62.1	0.686
Buffalo-Niagara Falls, NY	38.4	59.8	0.653

Source: U. S. Department of Labor. Bureau of Labor Statistics, *Geographic Profile of Employment and Unemployment: 1991.*

ployment rates ranged from a high of 75.8 percent in Hartford to a low of 38.4 percent in Buffalo-Niagara Falls. Buffalo-Niagara Falls was the only place in which the African American employment-to-population ratio was under 40 percent. In 9 MSAs, the African American employment-to-population ratio was less than 50 percent and in 20 MSAs it was less than 55 percent. There are only 6 MSAs with African American employment-to-population ratios of 65 percent and above.[7] African Americans have their lowest employment rates in the large metropolitan areas of the Northeast and the industrial heartland in the Midwest. African Americans did well generally in the moderate-sized areas of the West and the South where African Americans had employment-to-population ratios that were lower than whites. The average employment-to-population ratio for African Americans was 56.3 percent and for whites, it was 64.2 percent. Whites had only 2 MSAs, New York and Ft. Lauderdale, with employment-to-population ratios with less than 55 percent, none under 50 percent. On the other hand, the white employment-to-population ratio was higher than 65 percent in 18 MSAs.

Based on the B/W value of less than 2, African Americans generally had lower employment-to-population ratios than did whites in most MSAs. The B/W index ranged from a low of 0.653 in Buffalo-Niagara Falls to a high of 1.175 in Hartford. The B/W index was under 0.75 in 6 MSAs, 11 areas were under 0.85, 14 MSAs under 0.95, and 7 under 1.0. The employment situation in some MSAs worsened somewhat during the course of the year. In the 41 MSAs for which 1990 data were available, the employment-to-population ratio for African Americans increased in 17, decreased in 23 and remained the same in the rest.

As can be seen in Table 5.7, African American unemployment rates ranged from a low of 4.6 percent in Phoenix to a high of 22.3 percent in Detroit. African American unemployment rates were over 20 percent in 4 MSAs. The unemployment rate was greater than 14 percent in 13 areas, and over 10 percent in 19 places. The unemployment rates were lower than 8 percent in 4 areas. The highest unemployment rates for African Americans were in the big, older metropolitan areas of the Northeast and Midwest industrial heartland. African Americans did well in the newer, more moderate-sized economically diverse areas of the South and West. African Americans had higher unemployment rates in most MSAs than whites. The unemployment rates averages were 12.6 percent for African Americans and 5.7 percent for whites. Whites have no MSAs with an unemployment rate over 10 percent and only 4 areas with unemployment rates of at least 8 percent. White unemployment rate was less than 6 percent in 28 places.

As measured by a value of B/W greater than 1, African Americans usually had higher unemployment rates than whites in most places. The B/W index ranged from a low of 0.807 in Phoenix to a high of 5.583 in Milwaukee. The

Milwaukee B/W indicates that African Americans in the big industrial cities were at least five times more likely than whites to be unemployed. In addition to Phoenix, there were two other areas in the table which had B/W indexes of less than 1.0, 9 MSAs had B/W indexes of less than 2.0, 22 places had less than 3.0 and 9 places had over 3.0. African Americans had lower unemployment rates than whites in only 3 of the 43 MSAs in the table. The unemployment rates for African Americans increased in 25 MSAs and decreased in the other 16. Inequality in unemployment rates as measured by the B/W indicator went down between 1990 and 1991 in more places and increased in 12. This phenomenon was caused by higher relative increases or lower relative declines in white unemployment rates. Certainly the data revealed that inequality in unemployment was still rampant in most areas. There were no MSAs with an unemployment rate for whites that were over 10 percent and only 4 areas with unemployment rates of at least 8 percent. The white unemployment rate was less than 6 percent in 28 places.

As measured by a value of B/W greater than 1, African Americans usually had higher unemployment rates than whites in most places. The B/W index ranged from a low of 0.807 in Phoenix to a high of 5.583 in Milwaukee. The Milwaukee B/W indicates that African Americans in the big industrial cities were at least five times more likely than whites to be unemployed. In addition to Phoenix, there were two other areas in the table which had B/W indexes of less than 1.0, 9 MSAs had B/W indexes of less than 2.0, 22 places had less than 3.0 and 9 places had over 3.0. African Americans had lower unemployment rates than whites in only 3 of the 43 MSAs in the table. The unemployment rates for African Americans increased in 25 MSAs and decreased in the other 16. Inequality in unemployment rates as measured by the B/W indicator went down between 1990 and 1991 in more places and increased in 12. This phenomenon was caused by higher relative increases or lower relative declines in white unemployment rates.

Table 5.8 displays data on the distribution of employed African Americans and whites based on major occupational categories. The table shows the persistence of occupational disadvantages in the post-Reagan era. It should be noted that African Americans' disadvantage is understated by the fact that the broad occupational categories included some very disparate groupings. For example, the sales category includes cashiers at department stores in the same broad grouping as high-powered industry representatives.

The pay and condition of labor vary widely among these occupations and African Americans tended to be concentrated in the least desirable subgroups in each broad category. However, as seen from the table, African Americans were under represented in the most desirable occupations and over represented in the less desirable occupations.

Table 5.8. Occupational Percent Distribution of Employed Workers, 1991

	Male			Female		
	Black	*White*	*B/W*	*Black*	*White*	*B/W*
Exec., Admin., & Managerial	7.2	14.7	0.49	7.2	12.0	0.60
Professional Specialty	6.7	12.6	0.53	11.5	16.1	0.71
Technicians & Related Support	2.3	3.0	0.77	3.4	3.5	0.97
Sales Occupations	6.2	11.8	0.53	9.4	13.3	0.71
Administrative Support	8.9	5.4	1.65	26.3	27.9	0.94
Private Household	0.1	—	NA	2.7	1.3	2.08
Protective Service	4.6	2.6	1.77	1.3	0.5	2.60
Other Service	14.2	6.4	2.22	23.6	14.8	1.59
Precision Pro., Craft, & Repair	15.2	19.5	0.78	2.2	2.1	1.05
Mach. Operators, Assem., & Inspectors	10.0	7.0	1.43	9.2	5.2	1.77
Trans. and Material Movers	11.9	6.6	1.80	1.1	0.8	1.38
Handlers, Cleaners, Helpers, Laborers	9.4	5.7	1.65	1.9	1.5	1.27
Farming, Forestry, & Fishing	3.5	4.7	0.74	0.3	1.2	0.25

Source: U.S. Department of Labor, Bureau of Labor Statistics, *Employment and Earnings,* January 1992.

African American men were only half as likely as white men to be employed in three top job categories: executive, administrative, and managerial; professional and related specialties; and sales occupations. African American women were between 60 percent and 71 percent as likely as white women to be employed in these occupations. African American men were also only about three-fourths as likely to be employed in technical and related support, or precision production, craft, and repair occupations. African American men were more likely to be employed in all of the other occupations except farming. These other occupations tended to be more risky, dirty, subservient, lower paying, and less desirable. Also as displayed on the list, African American women were over represented in the less desirable occupations. The under representation of African American men in high-paying jobs caused the aggregate gap of 1.412 million good jobs. The under representation of African American women in good jobs resulted in an aggregate gap of 897,000 higher-paying jobs. The total aggregate gap for African American men and women was 2,309,000 good jobs.

AFRICAN AMERICAN INCOME AND POVERTY LEVEL

Effect on Income

The impact of the wide gaps in unemployment, employment, and occupational distributions resulted in lower income and poverty levels for African

Americans. Table 5.9 presents the data on aggregate and per capita income for African Americans. In 1991, the Bureau of Census reported that the per capita income of the African American was $9,170 in a population of 31,438,000, which means that the total income of African Americans was $288.3 billion. African Americans were 12.5 percent of the total population of 251,434,000. African Americans received only 7.84 percent of the total income of $3,675.2 billion, while white Americans received $15,510 in per capita income. The income equality B/W index was 59.1, which means that African Americans received 50 cents for every dollar received by whites. African Americans had $6,340 less income per capita than whites. In the aggregate, African American income was $199.3 billion less than would have been required to have per capita income parity. As displayed in Table 5.9, income for African Americans and whites declined for the second straight year in 1991 after reaching its highest level in 1989. African American per capita income declined 4.6 percent during the period 1990 to 1991 and white per capita income declined 5.2 percent during the same period.

During the first period of Reagan's administration, from 1981 to 1982, there were declines in African American aggregate and per capita income. The pre-Reagan era, from 1975 to 1979, experienced a constant increase in per capita and aggregate income. During the Reagan and post-Reagan years, African American aggregate income increased by 37 percent and the per capita income increased by 15 percent. The increase in aggregate and per capita income during the pre-Reagan years was significantly higher than the Reagan and post-Reagan years. The aggregate income was 54 percent and per capita income was 31 percent. African American income growth slowed down significantly during the Reagan and post-Reagan years. However, as revealed by the inequality index and the two gaps, inequality worsened during the Reagan and post-Reagan era. During the 1970s, African Americans made a little progress, by comparison with the end of the 1980s, in improving relative equality as measured by the B/W index. The Reagan administration definitely impeded the African American modest growth in per capita income inequality.

Perusing Table 5.10 shows the relative median incomes of African Americans and whites. In 1991, African American male and female income recipients had less median income than white male and female recipients. It should be noted that both African American and white male workers had incomes during the post-Reagan years that were lower than they were during the pre-Reagan era. The two groups' median income also declined during 1989, 1990, and 1991. The median incomes of both male groups were lower at the end of the Reagan era than they were at the beginning of the Reagan years. As seen

Table 5.9. Per Capita Income, Aggregate Income, and Income Gaps

	Aggregate Black Income (Billions)	Black	Per Capita Income *	White	B/W	Parity Per Capita	Aggregate Gaps (Billions)
1991	288.3	$9,170		$15,510	59.1	6,340	199.3
1990	290.3	9,396		15,907	59.1	6,511	201.2
1989	292.0	9,608		16,362	58.7	6,754	205.3
1988	284.7	9,522		15,999	59.5	6,477	193.7
1987	269.6	9,166		15,758	58.2	6,592	193.9
1986	259.1	8,956		15,350	58.3	6,394	185.0
1985	247.1	8,658		14,773	58.6	6,115	174.5
1984	231.6	8,228		14,340	57.4	6,112	172.1
1983	218.4	7,870	(7,865)	13,846	56.8	5,976	165.8
1982	208.2	7,636	(7,561)	13,573	56.3	5,937	161.9
1981	208.5	7,753	(7,679)	13,573	57.1	5,820	156.5
1980	210.3	7,950	(7,939)	13,625	58.3	5,675	150.1
1979	212.9	8,179	(8,336)	13,940	58.7	5,761	150.0
1978	203.8	8,140	(8,420)	13,715	59.4	5,575	139.6
1977	191.3	7,702	(8,030)	13,146	58.6	5,444	135.2
1976	184.4	7,535	(7,860)	12,740	59.1	5,205	127.4
1975	174.0	7,203	(7,519)	12,292	58.6	5,089	123.0
1974	169.7	7,133	(7,505)	12,274	58.1	5,141	122.3
1973	171.3	7,275	(7,724)	12,584	57.8	5,309	125.0
1972	163.6	7,055	(7,486)	12,172	58.0	5,117	118.6
1971	149.3	6,516	(6,932)	11,364	57.3	4,848	111.1
1970	143.1	6,164	(6,554)	10,061	55.7	4,897	113.7,
1969	137.0	6,091	(6,554)	10,972	55.5	4,881	109.8
1968	127.8	5,708	(6,183)	10,419	54.8	4,711	105.5
1967	115.9	5,260	(5,718)	9,770	53.8	4,510	99.4

Aggregate income = per capita * population
*Numbers in parentheses ( ) represent historical income figures adjusted based on unrevised consumer price index.
Source: U. S. Department of Labor, Bureau of the Census, *Money Income of Households, Families, and Persons in the United States: 1991,* August 1992, Series P-60, No. 180.

Table 5.10.   Median Income of Persons with Income by Race and Sex

	Male			Female		
	Black	White	BM	Black	White	B/W
1991	$12,962	$21,395	60.6	$8,816	$10,721	82.2
1990	13,409	22,061	60.8	8,678	10,751	80.7
1989	13,850	22,916	60.4	8,650	10,777	80.3
1988	13,866	22,979	60.3	8,461	10,480	80.7
1987	13,446	22,666	59.3	8,331	10,199	81.7
1986	13,449	22,443	59.9	8,160	9,643	84.6
1985	13,630	21,659	62.9	7,945	9,312	85.3
1984	12,385	21,586	57.4	8,080	9,109	88.7
1983	12,335	21,092	58.5	7,615	8,912	85.4
1982	12,591	21,011	59.9	7,498	8,501	88.2
1981	12,851	21,611	59.5	7,412	8,343	88.8
1980	13,254	22,057	60.1	7,580	8,187	92.6
1979	14,019	22,648	61.9	7,358	8,085	91.0
1978	13,844	23,110	59.9	7,480	8,307	90.0
1977	13,560	22,850	59.3	7,446	8,622	86.4
1976	13,179	22,785	60.2	7,791	8,268	94.2
1975	13,475	22,538	59.8	7,530	8,288	90.9
1974	14,397	23,235	62.0	7,385	8,180	90.3
1973	14,754	24,392	60.5	7,352	8,146	90.3
1972	14,519	23,970	60.6	7,497	8,025	93.4
1971	13,639	22,870	59.6	6,778	7,736	87.6
1970	13,709	23,121	59.3	6,803	7,473	91.0
1969	13,603	23,386	58.2	6,361	7,543	84.3
1968	13,432	22,641	59.3	5,957	7,511	79.3
1967	12,554	21,935	57.2	5,478	6,960	78.7

Source: U. S. Department of Commerce, Bureau of the Census, *Money Income of Households, Families, and Persons in the United States: 1991*, Series P-60, No. 180, August 1992.

from the B/W index, inequality is very marked among males. In 1991, African American male median income was $12,962 compared to $21,395 for white males. The B/W index shows that the average African American male income recipient received only 61 cents for every dollar received by the average white male. This high degree of inequality continued throughout the Reagan and post-Reagan years. Income inequality between African American and white males was higher during the Reagan and post-Reagan years than during the pre-Reagan era. However, the fact remains that inequality persisted and no attempt was made to improve the level of income inequality for African American males.

Both African American and white female incomes increased throughout the whole period. In 1991, the median income of African American female recipients was $8,816 compared to $10.721 for white females. African American female income had increased from $7,580 in 1980, an increase of 16.3 percent. White female income increased from $8,187 in 1980, an increase of 31 percent. African American female income increased by 19.2 percent during the pre-Reagan years, white female income increased by 8.5 percent during the pre-Reagan era. Although both female group incomes improved better than males, the data showed that the income gaps were still wide. It should be noted that the incomes of African American females were significantly less than the incomes of white females. The B/W index for 1991 revealed that African American females received only about 82 cents for every dollar received by white females. The B/W index for males was 60.6 in 1991; hence, it is clear that the racial inequality by this measure between females was less than it was between males. Certainly, racial inequality increased significantly for females during the Reagan and post-Reagan era. The B/W index for females was 92.6 percent in 1980, which dropped to 82.2 percent in 1991. This shows a significant increase in racial inequality in income for females and reverses all of the gains made during the 1970s in reducing the racial gap in female incomes. However, the lower average incomes of African American males and females were another important reason why the income gap persists.

Effect on Family Income

Perusal of Table 5.11 shows data on median family income. The median family income of African Americans was $21,548 and the median family income of whites was $37,783. The data reveals that African American family income, at best, stagnated during the Reagan and post-Reagan years. The African American family income was lower during the decade of the 1980s than it was in the decade of the 1970s. The average median income of African Americans during and after Reagan was $21,189, while the median family income for whites averaged $37,368 during and after the Reagan era, which was an increase of $1,764 from the $35,604 of the pre-Reagan average.

Based on the B/W measurement, inequality in family income substantially increased in absolute and relative terms. The median family income gaps were basically larger during the Reagan and post-Reagan years than the pre-Reagan period. The gap was $15,275 in 1980 and $16,235 in 1991. Throughout the 11 years of Reagan and post-Reagan, the average gap was $16,179 compared to the median family income gap average of $14,568 in the 11-pre-Reagan years. The aggregate gap increased from $95.5 billion in 1980 to $136.6 billion in 1991. During and after Reagan, the aggregate gap averaged about $120.1 billion and about $82.6 billion in the pre-Reagan years. The B/W index indicates that relative inequality was also higher during the Reagan and post-Reagan eras.

Table 5.11. Median Family Income and Inequality Indicators for Selected Years

	Black	Median Family Income*	White	B/W	Median Income Gap	Aggregate Gap (Billions)
1991	$21,548		$37,783	57.0	$16,235	136.6
1990	22,325		38,468	58.9	16,143	132.2
1989	22,197		39,514	56.2	17,317	139.4
1988	22,254		39,047	57.0	16,793	127.9
1987	22,068		38,828	56.8	16,760	127.4
1986	21,877		38,286	57.1	16,409	120.3
1985	21,248		36,901	57.6	15,653	114.0
1984	20,228	(20,230)	36,293	55.7	16,065	112.3
1983	19,912	(19,901)	35,331	56.4	15,419	106.6
1982	19,373	(19,183)	35,052	55.3	15,679	105.5
1981	20,054	(20,862)	35,550	56.4	15,496	99.2
1980	20,974	(20,944)	36,249	57.9	15,275	95.5
1979	21,302	(21,712)	37,619	56.6	16,317	98.2
1978	21,951	(22,707)	37,063	59.2	15,112	88.8
1977	20,609	(21,488)	36,076	57.1	5,467	88.1
1976	21,191	(22,107)	35,625	59.5	14,434	83.2
1975	21,276	(22,211)	34:578	61.5	13,302	77.3
1974	21,010	(22,107)	35,186	59.7	14,176	80.8
1973	20,975	(22,273)	36,344	57.7	15,369	84.1
1972	21,056	(22,341)	35,427	59.4	14,371	76.9
1971	20,351	(21,653)	33,725	60.3	13,374	70.1
1970	20,707	(22,019)	33,756	61.3	13,049	65.9
1969	20,738	(22,283)	33,856	61.3	13,118	65.7
1968	19,364	(20,979)	32,287	60.0	12,923	60.6
1967	18,291	(19,882)	30,895	59.2	12:604	58.9

Note: Aggregate gap is defined as the difference in mean income (not shown) times the number of black families (not shown). Median family income is in 1991 CPI-U adjusted dollars.

*Numbers in parentheses ( ) represent historical income figures adjusted based on unrevised consumer price index.

Source: U. S. Department Of Commerce, Bureau of the Census, *Money Income of Households, Families, and Persons in the United States: 1991,* Series P-60, No. 180.

The B/W index value was 57.0 in 1991. In 1980, the B/W index was 57.9. The inequality between African American and white family incomes during and after Reagan was certainly higher than they were before Reagan. Throughout the Reagan and post-Reagan years, the African American families lost income of about $1.32 trillion in total.

Table 5.12 presents data on the distribution of family income. The proportion of African American families receiving incomes under $10,000 rose from 24.1 percent in 1988 and 23.4 percent in 1989 to 26.4 percent in 1991. African American families receiving income under $5,000 per year rose from 9.7 percent to 11.4 percent during this period. However, the proportion receiving very high incomes, over $50,000 per year, declined from 17.4 percent in 1988

Table 5.12. Percentage of Families Receiving Income: Selected Ranges by Race

	Under $5,000		$5,000–$9,999		Less than $10,000		$10,000–$14,999		$10,000–$34,999		$35,000 $100,000+		$50,000 $100,000+		$100,000 and over	
	Black	White	Black	White	Black	White	Black	White	Black	White	Black	White	Black	White	Black	White
1991	11.4	2.5	15.0	4.8	26.4	7.3	11.1	6.7	44.0	38.3	29.6	54.4	14.9	34.1	1.4	6.1
1990	10.9	2.3	13.8	4.4	24.7	6.7	11.2	6.7	44.2	38.0	31.2	55.3	16.1	34.7	1.5	6.6
1989	9.7	2.3	13.7	4.5	23.4	6.8	12.6	6.5	45.2	36.7	31.4	56.7	16.8	36.0	1.6	7.0
1988	9.7	2.3	13.7	4.5	23.4	6.8	12.9	6.5	44.6	37.4	31.4	55.6	17.4	34.9	2.1	6.3
1987	9.9	2.3	14.8	4.8	24.7	7.1	11.7	6.2	45.1	36.9	30.1	55.9	15.8	34.8	1.9	6.1
1986	10.0	2.6	14.1	4.9	24.1	7.5	12.2	6.6	45.4	37.8	30.5	54.6	15.3	33.6	1.4	5.9
1985	9.2	2.6	15.2	5.2	24.4	7.8	12.1	6.8	47.1	39.4	28.6	52.7	13.7	31.9	1.1	5.2
1984	9.9	2.6	15.5	5.1	25.4	7.7	13.7	7.2	48.4	40.1	26.2	52.1	13.2	30.9	0.9	4.8
1983	10.3	2.9	16.4	5.3	26.7	8.2	12.8	7.3	47.5	41.5	25.8	50.2	11.7	29.9	0.5	4.3
1982	9.4	2.9	17.4	5.3	26.8	5.1	13.6	7.4	47.9	42.0	25.3	49.9	10.2	29.3	0.5	4.1
1981	8.4	2.4	16.2	5.0	24.6	7.4	13.5	7.2	49.2	41.9	26.2	50.7	11.6	28.5	0.3	3.5
1980	7.9	2.1	15.1	5.0	23.0	7.1	13.9	6.9	49.9	41.0	27.0	51.8	12.5	29.0	0.6	3.6
1979	7.1	1.9	15.1	4.4	22.2	6.3	13.8	6.7	49.3	39.6	29.6	54.1	13.2	30.5	0.6	4.2
1978	6.7	2.0	15.5	4.4	22.2	6.4	12.3	7.2	49.3	40.3	28.3	53.3	13.4	29.9	0.6	4.1
1977	6.8	2.0	14.8	4.7	21.6	6.7	15.1	7.4	52.5	41.9	25.9	51.5	11.3	28.2	0.6	3.5
1976	5.3	1.8	16.3	4.9	21.6	6.7	14.4	7.6	52.1	42.5	26.2	50.8	10.7	27.0	0.5	3.2
1975	5.8	1.9	16.0	5.2	21.9	7.1	14.6	7.9	52.9	44.0	25.4	49.9	9.6	25.1	0.4	2.9
1974	5.8	1.9	15.4	4.5	21.2	6.4	14.3	7.3	53.8	43.6	25.0	49.9	10.3	26.4	0.4	3.1
1973	6.1	1.8	14.9	4.8	21.0	6.6	15.2	7.0	54.5	42.0	24.5	51.5	10.0	27.6	0.6	3.4
1972	6.2	2.0	15.5	5.0	21.7	7.0	14.0	6.9	52.9	42.8	25.3	50.3	10.2	26.2	0.6	3.2
1971	6.0	2.3	16.2	5.4	22.2	7.7	13.7	7.2	55.5	45.8	22.3	46.4	8.7	22.6	0.4	2.4
1970	7.3	2.4	14.6	5.5	21.9	7.9	13.5	7.0	55.4	45.7	22.7	46.5	8.9	22.6	0.3	2.5
1969	7.3	2.3	13.1	5.5	20.4	7.9	15.1	6.9	59.3	45.6	21.1	46.7	7.7	22.5	0.2	2.4
1968	7.1	2.5	14.6	5.4	21.7	7.9	16.3	7.6	58.2	49.3	20.1	43.9	7.1	19.6	0.3	1.9
1967	9.4	2.8	17.1	6.4	25.5	9.2	15.1-	7.3	57.8	50.5	16.7	40.3	5.9	17.5	0.5	2.0

Note: Total will not equal 100.0 due to overlap of categories. Data are 1991 CPI-U-XI adjusted dollars.
Source: U.S. Department of Labor, Bureau of Labor Statistics, *Money Income of Households, Families, and Persons in the United States: 1991,* Series P-60, No. 180, August 1992.

to 14.8 percent in 1991. There was also evidence of inequality in the income distribution. African Americans were 4.56 times more likely than whites to have very low incomes, under $5,000. African American families were less than 23 percent as likely to have incomes over $100,000. In 1991, there were 7,716,000 African American families; about 1.47 million African American families had incomes below $10,000 and 1.49 million African American families had incomes over $50,000.

During the 12 years of Reagan and Bush, the rate of African Americans receiving low incomes increased. The rate of families receiving incomes less than $10,000 averaged 25.0 percent, while the average for the 11 years of pre-Reagan was 21.9 percent. The average proportion of whites receiving such low incomes increased slightly, from 6.9 percent to 7.4 percent, during the Reagan and Bush period. Although the average proportion of whites receiving these high incomes also increased absolutely, from 40.1 percent to 43.7 percent. The relative gap was on the average lower during the Reagan and post-Reagan years. Obviously, the bottom of the African American income distribution was lower during the Reagan and Bush years but, on the other hand, the top was higher. Inequality within the African American population increased.

Analyzing the data in Table 5.13 shows the Reagan and post-Reagan era income at different levels of the African American income distribution. The data in Table 5.13 presents the mean income distribution. It is a fact, therefore, that the income of African American families of every level was significantly lower than the income for whites at the corresponding level. The African American families' mean income in 1991 at the lowest level was significantly lower than the income for whites at the corresponding level. The African American families' mean income in 1991 at the lowest level was only $4,369 compared to $11,407 for whites. The top 5 percent of African Americans had mean incomes of $95,201 compared to the top 5 percent of whites.

During the 12 years of the Reagan and Bush era, the data in Table 5.13 reveals that the higher the income class, the more the mean income had risen since the 1980s. Actually, since 1980, the incomes of the two lowest groups of African Americans declined by about 21 percent for the bottom fifth and 8 percent for the second fifth. At the other end, the mean incomes of the top three levels increased by 3 percent, 6 percent, and 11 percent, respectively. The mean income of the top 5 percent increased by about 17 percent over the same period. This proved that during and after Reagan, the poor got poorer while the rich got richer. Income inequality continued to be substantial at all levels during and after the Reagan period. Certainly, inequality was greater for the poor. The B/W index reveals that African Americans at the bottom had

Table 5.13.   Mean Income of Families at Selected Positions of the Income Distribution 1991, 1990, 1980, 1970

	Black	*White*	*Black/White*
1991			
Lowest Fifth	$4,369	$11,407	38.3%
Second	11,594	24,997	46.4
Third	21,585	37,773	57.1
Fourth	35,022	53,913	65.0
Highest Fifth	65,286	98,313	66.4
Top 5%	95,201	152,297	62.5 .
1990			
Lowest Fifth	$4,721	$11,834	39.9%
Second	12,325	25,778	47.8
Third	22,394	38,568	58.1
Fourth	36,295	54:723	66.3
Highest Fifth	67,860	101,161	67.1
Top 5 %	99:563	159,082	62.6
1980			
Lowest Fifth	$5,519	$11,455	48.2%
Second	12,546	24,615	51.0
Third	20,966	36,234	57.9
Fourth	33,193	49,593	66.9
Highest Fifth	58,564	84,459	66.3
Top 5 %	82,510	124,763	65.3
1970			
Lowest Fifth	$5,619	$10,909	51.5%
Second	12:990	23,721	54.8
Third	20,641	33,476	61.7
Fourth	30,604	44:712	68.4
Highest Fifth	52,867	76,724	68.9
Top 5%	74,580	117:172	63.7

Source: U.S. Department Of Commerce, Bureau of the Census, *Money Income of Households, Families, and Persons in the United States: 1991,* August 1992, Series P-60, No. 180.

only 38.3 percent as high mean incomes as white families at the bottom, and African American families in the second fifth had only 46.5 percent of the income of corresponding white families. As can be seen in the table, by comparing the 1980 and 1991 B/W indexes, the degree of inequality for poorer African American families worsened.

The so-called safety net provided little or no protection for poor African Americans during and after the Reagan years. It is apparent, therefore, that inequality was very high for African Americans on the overall. However, a comparison of the data for 1991 and 1980 indicates that inequality rose for the top of the distribution as well as during after the Reagan years. Hence, over the 11 years of Reagan and post-Reagan, inequality increased for all African Americans throughout the income distribution.

Table 5.14 displays data on family income by region. Family income for both African Americans and whites declined in all regions during 1991. African Americans of the western region had the highest income, $28,298. The next highest African American region was the Northeast with an income of $20,860, followed by the South with an income of $20,124. African American incomes were significantly lower than white incomes in all the regions. Equality was greatest in the West, where the index of equality was 75.2 percent. Inequality was highest in the Midwest with a B/W index of only 54.6 percent. African American median income was 61.1 percent of white median income in the Northeast and 57.1 percent of white income in the South. Over the 11 years of the Reagan and post-Reagan era, African American family incomes increased relative to 1980 income in the Northeast and the South, was constant in the West, and declined in the Midwest. The average median family income was substantially higher in the Northeast, $24,044 during and after Reagan compared to $22,927 during pre-Reagan, and the West was at $27,478 compared to $24,732 during the same periods. The average income in the South was a little higher at $19,842 during and after Reagan compared to $19,530 during the pre-Reagan period. The average income in the Midwest was substantially lower, $20,076 compared to $26,047 during the same period.

Family income inequality as measured by the B/W index was on the average higher in the Midwest, South, and Northeast during and after Reagan than it was in the pre-Reagan era. The average inequality index in the South, during pre-Reagan was 59.2 percent and 57.1 percent during and after the Reagan period. The average fell from 61.1 percent to 59.0 percent in the Northeast. Inequality was highest in the Midwest, where the B/W index decreased from 70.1 percent to 53.7 percent. Apparently, the Midwest was the most equal region in the pre-Reagan era, but during and after the Reagan years, it was the most unequal region. However, inequality declined based on the B/W measure in the West as the index increased from an average of 67.9 percent in the pre-Reagan years to 72.3 percent during the Reagan and post-Reagan period.

Poverty

As discussed in the previous section, labor market earnings determine the amount of income received by African Americans. Labor market earnings depend on the national employment and unemployment rates. However, the persisting inequality in income accounts for the large level of poverty among

Table 5.14. Median Family Income by Region

	Northeast			Midwest			South			West		
	Black	White	B/W	Black	White	B/W	Black	White	B/W	Black	White	B/W
1991	$25,533	$41,815	61.1	$20,860	$38,224	54.6	$20,124	$35,226	57.1	$28,298	$37,610	75.2
1990	25,720	42,821	60.1	21,375	38,943	54.9	21,680	35,683	60.8	29,123	38,387	75.9
1989	27,889	45,023	61.9	20,102	39,310	51.1	20,901	36,180	57.8	28,196	39,700	71.0
1988	28,249	43,350	65.2	20,147	39,496	51.0	20,853	36,907	56.5	29,801	38,610	77.2
1987	24,836	42,410	58.6	20,124	38,612	52.1	20,204	36,252	55.7	24,774	39,047	63.4
1986	25,987	41,498	62.6	21,604	37,968	56.9	18,269	32,336	56.5	27,562	39,047	70.6
1985	22,892	39,861	57.4	20,197	36,663	55.1	20,020	34,308	58.4	30,953	38,277	80.9
1984	21,401	38,940	55.0	18,833	36,289	51.9	19,484	34,154	57.0	25,181	37,372	67.4
1983	21,317	37,953	56.2	17,843	34,916	51.1	18,9I9	33,455	56.5	24,911	35,569	70.0
1982	20,634	36,152	57.1	17,328	34,678	50.0	19,256	34,160	56.4	28,373	37,446	75.8
1981	20,026	37,321	53.7	22,428	36,107	62.1	18,568	33,333	55.7	25,081	36,769	68.2
1980	21,827	37,405	58.4	23,242	36,928	62.9	19,245	34,143	56.4	28,357	37,426	75.8
1979	22,129	39,268	56.4	23,977	38,823	61.8	19,764	34,684	57.0	24,148	38,729	62.4
1978	24,156	38,832	62.2	28,339	39,409	71.9	20,3H9	35,488	57.5	22,380	39,026	57.3
1977	22,165	37,287	59.4	23,038	37,134	62.0	19,314	33,880	57.0	21,372	36,604	58.4
1976	22,303	36,286	61.5	24,954	37,455	66.6	19,550	33,050	59.2	22,592	36,093	62.6
1975	19,800	35,996	55.0	28,372	35,986	79.8	21,222	31,694	67.0	24,943	35,138	71.0
1974	22,110	37,590	58.8	31,646	36,777	86.0	23,629	31,924	74.0	26,802	35,100	76.4
1973	22,398	38,176	58.7	26,285	37,882	69.4	18,566	33,207	55.9	23,757	36,534	65.0
1972	23,976	37,753	63.5	25,516	36,648	69.6	17,678	32,102	55.1	25,501	35,964	70.9
1971	24,020	35,681	67.3	24,026	34,821	69.0	17,109	30,672	55.8	24,089	34,138	70.6
1970	27,316	38,355	71.2	27,119	36,923	73.4	18,363	32,468	56.6	28,114	36,482	77.1
1969	23,890	35,485	67.3	26,708	35,239	75.8	17,239	30,296	56.9	26,556	35,250	75.3
1968	23,342	33,671	69.3	24,964	33,450	74.1	15,473	28,768	53.8	27,117	34,184	79.3
1967	21,177	32,489	65.2	24,021	31,330	76.7	14,832	27,611	53.7	24,430	33,048	73.9

Sources: U.S. Department of Labor, Bureau of the Census, *Money Income of Households, Families, and Persons in the United States, 1991,* Series P-60, No. 180. August 1992.

African Americans. Poverty is the lack of enough income to maintain the basic
level of living. Moreover, high unemployment rate and inequality in income explained high rate of poverty among African American during the Reagan era.

Tables 5.15, 5.16, and 5.17 provide data on the numbers of people living in
poverty and poverty rates for all persons, children, and persons in female-
headed families. The number of persons in poverty among African Americans
was significantly high in all the categories. The number of African Americans
in poverty was a total of 10,242,000. The number of children in poverty
among female-headed families was 65,557,000. In 1991, poverty rates rose
from 31.9 percent in 1990 to 32.7 percent in 1991. The poverty rate for children rose from 44.8 percent to 45.6 percent and (the poverty rate for individuals in female-headed families rose from 50.6 percent to 54.8 percent). The

Table 5.15.   Selected Poverty Rates by Race for Selected Years

	Persons in Poverty					
	Number (Millions)		Percent			Poverty Gap (Millions)
	Black	White	Black	White	B/W	
1991	10,242	23,747	32.7	11.3	2.9	6.70
1990	9,837	22,326	31.9	10.7	3.0	6.53
1989	9,302	20,785	30.7	10.0	3.1	6.28
1988	9,356	20,715	31.3	10.1	3.1	6.33
1987	9,520	21,195	32.4	10.4	3.1	6.33
1986	8,983	22,183	31.1	11.0	2.8	5.80
1985	8,983	22,860	31.3	11.4	2.7	5.67
1984	9,490	22,955	33.8	*11.5*	2.9	6.26
1983	9,882	23,984	35.7	12.1	3.0	6.53
1982	9,697	23,517	35.6	12.0	3.0	6.42
1981	9,173	21,553	34.2	11.2	3.1	6.17
1980	8,579	19,699	32.5	10.2	3.2	5.89
1979	8,050	17,214	31.0	8.9	3.5	5.73
1978	7,625	16,259	30.6	8.7	3.5	5.47
1977	7,726	16,416	31.3	8.9	3.5	5.54
1976	7,595	16,713	31.1	9.1	3.4	5.37
1975	7,545	17,770	31.3	9.7	3.2	5.20
1974	7,182	15,736	30.3	8.3	3.7	5.21
1973	7,388	15,142	31.4	8.3	3.8	5.43
1972	7,710	16,203	33.3	9.0	3.7	5.62
1971	7,396	17,780	32.5	9.9	3.3	*5.15*
1970	7,548	17,484	33.5	9.9	3.4	5.31
1969	7,095	16,659	32.5	9.5	3.4	5.06
1968	7,616	17,395	32.2	10.0	3.2	4.87
1967	8,486	18,983	39.3	11.0	3.6	6.11

Source: U.S. Department of Commerce, Bureau of the Census, *Poverty in the United States: 1991*, August
1992.

Table 5.16. Selected Poverty Rates by Race for Selected Years

	Children in Poverty					
	Number (Millions)		Percent			Poverty Gap (Millions)
	Black	White	Black	White	B/W	
1991	4,637	8,316	45.6	16.1	2.8	3.00
1990	4,550	8,232	44.8	15.9	2.8	2.88
1989	4,375	7,599	43.7	14.8	3.0	2.85
1988	4,296	7,435	43.5	14.5	3.0	2.81
1987	4,385	7,788	45.1	15.3	2.9	2.84
1986	4,148	8,209	43.1	16.1	2.7	2.56
1985	4,157	8,253	43.6	16.2	2.7	2.58
1984	4,413	8,472	46.6	16.7	2.8	2.80
1983	4,398	8,862	46.7	17.5	2.7	2.58
1982	4,472	8,678	47.6	17.0	2.8	2.84
1981	4,237	7,181	45.2	15.2	3.0	2.79
1980	3,961	6,193	42.3	13.9	3.0	2.64
1979	3,833	6,193	41.2	11.8	3.5	2.70
1978	3,830	5,831	41.5	11.3	3.7	2.77
1977	3,888	6,097	41.8	11.6	3.6	2.79
1976	3,787	6,189	40.6	11.6	3.5	2.69
1975	3,925	6,927	41.7	12.7	3.3	2.72
1974	3,755	6,223	39.8	11.2	3.6	2.68
1970	3,922	6,138	41.5	10.5	4.0	2.90

Source: U.S. Department of Commerce, Bureau of the Census, *Poverty in the United States: 1991,* August 1992.

B/W index measurement indicates the racial inequality was still high in 1991. For African Americans, the B/W index was 2.9 in 1991, meaning that African American children, the B/W index was 2.8, and for female-headed families, the B/W index was 1.7. As indicated in the 1991 columns of the three categories, the highest poverty gaps were in 1991. A record high of 6,700,000 additional African Americans, 3,000,000 additional children, and an excess of 2,790,000 persons in female-headed families were in poverty in 1991. These were poverty gaps, additional African Americans that were in poverty more than the number needed to equal the white poverty rates.

The Reagan administration's policy created an increase in African American poverty. During the 11 years of the Reagan and post-Reagan era, the annual average number of African Americans in poverty was 9,492,000, which was significantly higher than 7,668,000 people in poverty during the 11 pre-Reagan years. The African American poverty during and after Reagan was an average of 32.8 percent, significantly different from the average of 31.7 percent of the pre-Reagan era. The number and rates of poverty for children and persons in female-headed families during and after Reagan were also high on

Table 5.17.   Selected Poverty Rates by Race for Selected Years

	Persons Female—Headed Familes					
	Number (Millions)		Percent			Poverty Gap (Millions)
	Black	White	Black	White	B/W	
1991	6,557	6,806	54.8	31.5	1.7	2.79
1990	6,005	6,210	50.6	29.8	1.7	2.47
1989	5,530	5,723	49.4	28.1	1.8	2.38
1988	5,601	5,950	51.9	29.2	1.8	2.45
1987	5,789	5,989	54.1	29.6	1.8	2.62
1986	5,473	6,171	53.8	30.6	1.8	2.36
1985	5,342	5,990	53.2	29.8	1.8	2.35
1984	5,666	5,866	54.6	29.7	1.8	2.59
1983	5,736	6,017	57.0	31.2	1.8	2.60
1982	5,698	5,686	58.8	30.9	1.9	2.71
1981	5,222	5,600	56.7	29.8	1.9	2.48
1980	4,984	4,940	53.4	28.0	1.9	2.37
1979	4,816	4,375	53.1	25.2	2.1	2.53
1978	4,595	4,371	54.3	25.9	2.1	2.46
1977	4,712	4,474	55.3	26.8	2.1	2.37
1976	4,415	4,463	55.7	28.0	2.0	2.20
1975	4,168	4,577	54.3	29.4	1.8	1.91
1974	4,116	4,278	55.0	27.7	2.0	2.04
1973	4,064	4,003	56.5	28.0	2.0	2.05
1972	4,139	3,770	58.1	27.4	2.1	2.19
1971	3,587	4,099	56.1	30.4	1.8	1.64
1970	3,656	3,761	58.7	28.4	2.1	1.89
1969	3,225	3,577	58.2	29.1	2.0	1.61
1968	3,312	3,551	58.9	29.1	2.0	NA
1967	3,362	3,453	61.6	28.5	2.2	NA

Source: U.S. Department of Commerce, Bureau of the Census, *Poverty in the United States: 1991*, August 1992.

the average. African American children in poverty went up from an average of 3,863,000 to 4,370,000 during and after Reagan and the rate went up from an average of 41.3 percent to an average of 45.0 percent. The analysis for persons in African American female-headed families in poverty increased from an average of 4,296,000 to 5,693,000. The female-headed family poverty rate decreased slightly from 55.5 percent to 54.1 percent. It is apparent that there were increases in poverty during the Reagan era.

NOTES

1. The Congressional Black Caucus, *Quality of Life, Fiscal 1990 Alternative Budget* (Washington, D.C.: 1989) 1.

2. Lenneal J. Henderson, "Budget and Tax Strategy Implications for Blacks," *The State of Black America 1990*, New York, N.Y.: National Urban League, 1990) 60.

3. Henderson, Budget and Tax, 61.

4. William Darity and Samuel Myers, "Distress v. Dependency: Changing Income Support Programs," *The Urban League Review*, Vol. 10, No. 2 (Winter 1986–87): 24.

5. United States Department of Labor, Bureau of Labor Statistics, *Fact Sheet on Black and Hispanic Workers*, August 1994, 1.

6. Pre-Reagan era refers to the period from 1972 to 1980 and the post-Reagan era is from 1988 to 1992.

7. The six MSAs are Hartford, CT; Phoenix, AZ; Seattle, WA; Charlotte, NC; Dallas-Ft. Worth, TX; and Kansas City, KS.

Chapter Six

The Plight of African Americans

In need, might be a more appropriate way to describe the African American youths who are currently at risk. After years of little or no government policy, general public indifference and gross neglect, the issue of African American youths, especially the plight of poor African American youths in the inner cities, is a central issue of national interest and controversy. The decade of the 1960s produced a variety of federal government policies and programs designed to alleviate the problems of poverty, unemployment, education, substance dependency and crime in African American communities. During the 1960s, the predicament of African American youths received much attention in the national policy agenda, academic and media circles. The high rises in social indicators of physical and mental health, in drug abuse and crime, school dropouts and teenage pregnancy, have refocused attention on African American youth problems. The new generation of African American youth is becoming an endangered species.

Historically, African American youths have fared worse in the labor market than white youths. Over the past years, African American youths have experienced a remarkable deterioration in their labor market status. This condition reached a catastrophic proportion in the 1980s. For example, in 1983, 45 percent of African American youths, between the ages of 16 and 24, were unemployed compared to 19 percent of white youths. Also in 1983, while 64 percent of white youths were employed, only about 39 percent of African American youths were employed. African American youth employment crisis is particularly severe in the inner cities; in some cases the unemployment rate among African American youths is about 60 percent. The problem of unemployment has been particularly serious among male African American youths whose participation rate in the labor market declined from 59 percent in 1962 to 44 percent in 1985.[1] African American male youth accounted for 12 percent of all unemployed youth in 1987, about twice the national average of the teenage labor force.[2]

However, the official rate of youth unemployment understates the actual level of unemployment among African American youths in general, and males in particular, since it fails to include discouraged workers, those who have given up an active search for work and who are not included in the unemployment statistics. The dramatic increase of unemployment among African American youths during the 1980s has been attributed to some social and economic factors. Whatever factor contributes to the high level of unemployment among African American youths', the fact is that the costs of joblessness among African American youths can be calculated in more than economic terms. Situations that make it difficult or prevent African American youths from finding jobs, discourage their efforts toward economic independence, are more likely to promote their disaffection or alienation from the large society and may contribute to a range of social pathologies, including crime, substance abuse, and other lifestyles that are destructive to themselves and the society.

Teenagers between the ages of 16 and 19 constitute 6.7 percent of the economy's labor force but make up 17.9 percent of the official unemployment statistics. Unemployment among teenagers surged during the decade of the 1980s, resulting in an average high rate of 46 percent of unemployment among African American teenagers.[3] The above statistics did not include those who are underemployed or those who stopped looking for employment. The significantly less than average labor market participation among African American youths from poor families proves that there are no adequate policies and programs to address the African American youth employment problem.

Most of the existing youth programs are lacking in employment activities that could enhance youths' psychological functioning, such as apprenticeship programs. Most of the youth-oriented programs that were designed to compensate for the lack of work force participation have faced unanticipated problems that prevent them from reaching their objectives. Deep budget cuts in the 1980s, lack of management skills by program administrators and difficulty in communication within the organizational structure have impeded the progress of youth programs. Consequently, some youth programs failed to reach over 60 percent of the eligible youths.[4] The Reagan administration's Job Training Partnership Act (JTPA) served only the most qualified youth. Most employment agencies were supposed to serve economically and socially disadvantaged people, but under Reagan, the politically weak and disadvantaged received fewer services.

The failure of the education system, coupled with few employment opportunities and factors such as adolescent crime, and teenage unwed pregnancy, produce long-term social and economic problems. The devastation is so wide-spread that everyone is affected. The astronomical cost of supporting the un-productive and incarcerated weakens the American economy. Apparently, given the cost-effectiveness of many employment programs, the federal gov-ernment should direct more investment toward youth employment programs because they are worth the risk. So far, many programs that have been devel-oped to help socially and economically disadvantaged African-American youths have lacked substance.

Most of the sociocultural problems experienced by teenagers who are at risk are as a result of inequities in the educational and economic system. The federal government has the potential to develop programs that could reduce the structural causes or chain reaction of poverty and promote attitudes and behaviors that help families and communities function at an adequate level. In order to accomplish these objectives with poor African American youths, the federal government must understand the processes of African American youth development and the type of experiences and support required to be-come a responsible adult functioning in a predominantly white society. Poli-cymakers need to understand how institutions and conditions outside the African American youth and family operate to promote or to prevent poverty.

The unemployment rate among African American youths remained higher than the national unemployment rate not because of job shortage, but because of sociological rather than economical reasons. This view is the conventional wisdom. The economic solutions to unemployment problems are quite feasi-ble, but are under constraint by racist institutions, traditions, and conservative ideological public policy. African Americans youths are simply having a hard time finding jobs because of these constraints. Shortage of jobs in the inner cities is another problem facing African American youths. African American youths are concentrated in the central cities with declining job opportunities. They are simply finding fewer and fewer jobs in the inner cities. With limited employment opportunities, employers use several factors to determine who will be employed. Unfortunately for the African American youth, the em-ployment lottery is often rigged. Quite often, the color of the skin and family connections determine who gets the job.

Unemployment rates among African American youths contribute to the high poverty rate in the African American community. It is important for teenagers, especially poor youths, to have some form of work experience as teenagers; if they do not, they tend to have problems getting jobs as adults. Greater numbers of African American youths are entering their adult years with no job experience. For the simple fact that they are not in the labor mar-ket, their chances of being employed are substantially reduced; being an adult without job experience is a serious liability. Lack of job experience is a per-manent handicap for any unemployed African American youth. The unemployment problem has a big psychological effect on the expectations and attainments of African American children. The children feel that there is no reason to go to school or plan for a future if the generation ahead of them cannot succeed or show them the way to success. There is no future for them. The high unemployment rate among African American youths produced an underclass of people who experience prolonged and chronic unemployment.

African American youths are measuring barometers of change in labor market conditions for all black people because an individual's relative economic position is often established early in life. This simply means that success or failure during a person's early years can be translated into an indicator of success or failure at a later age for the group. It is hard to make up for a bad beginning. The vintage effect can be seen by comparing individual incomes, as they grow older. Comparing the earnings of African Americans to the earnings of whites will show that the older African Americans tend to have less relative earnings than whites.

FACTORS DETERMINING THE AFRICAN AMERICANS UNEMPLOYMENT RATES

Aggregate Demand

African American youth unemployment rates rise disproportionately with the rise of aggregate unemployment rates. Larson concluded that one percent rise in the overall unemployment rate leads to about three percent rise in youth's unemployment.[5] The major determinant of youth employment is aggregate demand for goods. Though the aggregate demand argument has failed to explain the reason for the wide racial gap in youth unemployment.

Labor Market Explanation

The key to explaining the high levels of unemployment rates among African American youths lies in the understanding of how labor market works. As seen in previous chapters, several supply side theory scholars argued that there is a monotonous labor market that is fundamentally competitive, which means that everyone in the labor market can compete for available jobs. These assumptions and observations are the conclusions reached by supply-siders, such as Smith and Welch.[6] It means that the high rate of unemployment among African American youths can lead to the assumption that African Americans are less interested in working, that they are less productive and less competitive in the labor market. Smith and Welch believed that an increase in education among African Americans will increase the returns from the investment in education and will result in African American economic progress. But the educational level of African Americans has greatly improved since the 1950s, while the unemployment rate has worsened.

With the exception of Smith and Welch, it is a fact clearly known that the African American economic progress has not improved significantly. During the 1980s, the supply side proponents attacked the federal government programs, arguing that they have robbed African Americans of their independence, self-respect and dignity. These supply-siders concluded that if African Americans cannot be employed or remain employed for a long time after years of government programs, then something must be dysfunctional about the African American culture.[7] What supply-siders failed to understand is that years of government programs are not the end of discrimination. The overwhelming evidence proves that African Americans basically earn less income from the performance of the same jobs that whites do. Seeborg, Seeborg and Zegeye supported this argument, in an analysis of the returns to CETA training by race.[8] The consequences of discrimination and unemployment are the reduction in the economic returns to education and training. There is a need for change in the demand for the African American labor force and effective government programs for changes in the characteristics of the African American labor force.

The assumption that the labor market is competitive is to assume that the major reason for high unemployment among African Americans does not exist. It is apparent that racial prejudice exists and that economic inequality exists in America today. The answer to the high unemployment rate cannot be found in a fair labor market. Several national polls constantly show that racial attitudes have improved over the past decades. If the general belief is that the labor market is fairly competitive, hence, there is no reason to argue that discrimination is the major cause for economic inequality.

Kenneth Arrow argued that with competitive labor markets and discrimination, employers act as if hiring African Americans of the same productivity as whites and at the same wage brings an added psychic cost. In such a situation, the discriminatory employer must pay whites more than African Americans. Hence, an all white labor force will result in a higher labor cost. Non-discriminatory employers will hire African Americans at lower wages and that will lead to lower labor costs to the advantage of the non-discriminatory employers. This labor market competitive theory predicts that there should be no economic inequality because the market will penalize discriminatory employers and reward non-discriminatory employers.[9] Since discrimination is the main cause for racial economic inequality, it is inappropriate to assume that a simple competitive labor market model rather than the discriminatory labor market is the explanation for the high unemployment rate among African Americans.

Labor market explanation is inadequate for explaining noncompetitive behavior. It is obvious that labor is neither simply allocated by prices in a free market, nor is it a commodity to be traded in a free commodity market like orange juice. These flaws in the supply side labor market theory are the fundamental reason for the Keynesian revolution in economic theory. The competitive labor market theory argued that wages are the primary means of allocating labor resources and that worker should be paid according to the color of their skin, gender, age, or religion. An analysis of the wages earned by workers by race proved that it is difficult to accept the labor market model as credible. Are Anglo-Americans males more productive and worth more than African Americans, Hispanics, Native Americans, Asians and women? Attempts to explain productivity as the sole reason for wage differences have failed. Several models of segmented or balkanized labor markets were based purely on observation of employment segregation among women and minorities and of earnings inequality.[10] These analyses concluded that employment segregation tend to reduce wages by limiting competition among the various groups.

A different way of examining employment inequality is by simply observing that the persistence of unemployment reflects a lack of competitive conditions in the labor market and then to model how jobs are rationed under certain conditions. Thurow stated, "Labor market is not primarily a bidding market for selling existing skills, but a training market where training slots must be allocated to different workers."[11] Thurow's analysis is based on the fact that productivity should be associated with the job not the employee, because the skills needed for high productivity can be easily learned from the job. The essence of going to school is not to acquire job skills, but to acquire knowledge and demonstrate an ability to be trained for a job. Most employers put more emphasis on job skills and experience than they put on education. We need to understand the labor market as it actually works, not as it might work under the conditions of perfect competition.

Education and Training

It is a fact clearly known that there are special advantages for youths who finish school. African American youths who finish school have more employment opportunities and earn more than high school dropouts. There are also racial differentials in the return from investment in education and training. The racial employment gap has widened for both in-school and out-of-school youths. White high school dropouts sometimes earn more than African American high school graduates. The nature of the high school program is also an important factor in getting a job. Meyer and Wise explained that the type of high school program that emphasizes reading, writing and arithmetic is very useful. The best preparation for competing in the job market as an adult is to work while going to high school and taking academic courses.[12]

A sound federal government-training program for youth unemployment should be designed for prolonged and intensive assistance for the truly disadvantaged youth. African American youths are truly in need. Federal government programs targeted to the chronically unemployed are difficult and expensive, but they are effective programs. An example of an effective youth unemployment program is the Job Corps, developed in 1964 by the Economic Opportunity Act and administered by the Department of Labor. In 1984, the annual cost of providing one training slot was $13,595. The cost per trainee was $5,595 and the average length of training was 12 months.[13] A study done by the Mathematical Policy Research concluded that the rate of return on the investment was about 46 percent.[14] Program participants received higher income because of the program effectiveness and they rapidly repaid society for the training cost as taxpayers.

President Reagan's Job Training Partnership Act shifted job training and placement for disadvantaged youths from the public to the private sector. JTPA provided job training for only 4 percent of eligible youths. Critics alleged that employers were training those workers who were most likely to be quickly employed rather than those who were mostly in need. Betsey et al. stated that a "problem cited in many reports was the tendency of program operators to serve the least disadvantaged of the eligible youth, leaving the most disadvantaged and needy without services."[15] This is called "creaming" and it is a widespread problem and reflects the effect of providing incentives for high number of placements as well as the difficulty of working with and locating the hard-core unemployed. Youths who most need the services are hard to recruit and place and consequently are ignored. During program service delivery, funds are often spent to maximize the number of successful placements made. Since agencies get paid according to the number of placements, they tend to work with the most employable youths, which guarantee them a high success rate of placement. As a result of creaming, those who are mostly in need of the JTPA program received the least help.

School Enrollment

A study of youth employment problem conducted by Mare and Winship revealed that changes in school enrollment patterns between African American youths and the white youths show a large part of widening employment gap.[16] The authors explained that in the 1970s school enrollment and armed service enlistments rose slightly among African Americans. However, they observed that this only account for part of the fall in the employment rate for those

African American youths in school, and may be a result rather than a cause. Causality is difficult to establish since reduced employment opportunity can cause youths to stay in school. Tom Larson studied the effects of school enrollment on employment across the nation and found no clear relationship.[17] It is also possible that the school dropout rate might be higher for youths if jobs were available. Changes in school enrollment patterns between the races cannot explain why the employment gap widens between African Americans and whites in school.

Industrial Structure

Tom Larson observed that industrial structure has a tremendous effect on youth employment.[18] Since 1979, some 85 percent of the new jobs have been in the lowest paying industries—personal, business and health services and retail trade. Simultaneously, jobs are shrinking in the high-wage goods-producing industries as well as in the highest paying service sector industries such as communications, transportation, and government. Overall, those industries with expanding employment paid annual wages and benefit nearly $9,000 less than those paid in industries with shrinking employment.

Population Size

It is believed that youth employment is reduced as the proportion of youths in the population increases.[19] If this is the case, the African American youth unemployment condition should have improved in the 1980s, since their relative size declined during this period. According to Larson, there is no evidence to support the argument that migrant workers are taking jobs away from African American youths.[20] On the other hand, Lieberson argued that a larger African American population should lead to greater economic equality between whites and blacks.[21] He stated that an increase in African American population would lead to greater employment opportunities in a wide range of occupations. The bigger the African American population, the better, because a large African American population would result in the demand for specialized skills and create a pool of African American teachers, business owners, lawyers, doctors and bankers. This will enable African Americans to move up the occupational ladder.

A large African American community can support the African American institutions and provide a strong base for political power. Larson's data analysis on large metropolitan areas concluded that African American youth employment was higher in those areas with greater percentage of African Americans in the 1970s and 1980s, that is, after controlling other unemployment factors.[22]

The summary of the argument is that where there is a greater desire to discriminate, there may be a counterbalancing force in the ability to discriminate as the African American community increases.

Residence

Residence is important to African American youth's employment. Jobs are disappearing in the inner cities and are moving to the suburbs and whites are filling the available jobs. Most of the manufacturing jobs in the inner cities have moved to other regions or to overseas. African American youths benefit more from employment growth in the inner city than employment growth in the suburbs. This proves that employers are discriminatory, reflecting both racial and employment practices not that transportation and information are severe problems.

Wage

President Reagan's nominee for the Equal Employment Opportunity Commission, Jeffrey Zuckerman, once said that African Americans should work for lower wages than whites in accepting jobs.[23] African Americans should be paid less than their value. This is already happening in the labor market and it is the main cause of inequality. How much worse can it get? The argument is that African American youths have lower productivity characteristics because of the likelihood that most of them attended inferior central city schools, and that they can only compete if they are paid lower wages. If productivity lies in the job and since most workers receive their training on the job, this should not matter much. In theory, creating a wage floor will tend to reduce the flexibility of wages and act as a restraint to employment during periods of high unemployment.

According to Brown the effect of increases in the minimum wage on unemployment is very modest.[24] For the total population, a 10 percent reduction in the minimum wage may reduce unemployment by one percent. African American youth wages are at a bare minimum. Reducing the minimum wage will greatly reduce the wage to low-wage workers. The advocates of lower wages for African American youths are saying that the reduction of their wages by 30 percent will increase their hours by three percentage points for a net loss in earnings, but an increase in employment. There is no clear evidence to support the argument that African American youth employment would increase due to a reduction in minimum wage, but they would definitely earn less. The real minimum wage has fallen greatly, yet there has not been any increase in the African American youth employment rate.

High income will stimulate demand for goods and services produced in youth sectors and hence benefit youths even if high-wage industries do not employ them directly. Any effort by the government or the labor market to reduce wages in areas of high unemployment could be counterproductive.

Poverty

Moynihan, commenting on what he considered to be modest success in the war on poverty, stated that poverty partly reflected "cultural and environmental obstacles to motivation."[25] Based on Lewis' study in Mexico, he concluded that a culture of poverty tends to perpetuate itself.[26]

The argument is that poor people are poor because they lack middle-class values, aspirations, and behavior. Piore argued that poor African American youths are unwilling to take up menial jobs or low wages.[27] Thus, the explanation for the widening employment gap is a result of changes in expectations and attitudes among African Americans, due to the civil rights movement and the surge in African Americans' pride. However, accurate studies revealed that poor African Americans are more willing to work than poor whites.[28] Borus also found that African Americans are willing to work at menial jobs at lower wages than white or Hispanic youths.[29] Borus' work refutes the culture-of-poverty theory. We must not continue to put down the victims of unemployment just because we lack the appropriate solutions for the youth unemployment problem.

Discrimination

Discrimination is the main cause of high unemployment among African American youths. There is strong evidence of persistent employment discrimination. Culp and Dunson studied employment discrimination in which African Americans and whites applied for the same jobs. They found that the applicants were treated differently, based on their race.[30]

Several statistical studies of the determinants of earnings continue to reveal that the huge earnings gap between blacks and whites reflects the presence of continued employment discrimination, not just differences in educational and training levels. The ongoing activities in retail employment practices present several problems for African Americans. Most small retail firms discriminate through the hiring of friends. This practice of discrimination and nepotism hurt African Americans the most since few own small retail businesses. The Reagan regime raised the small firm size requirement for filing for affirmative action practice. Such policy by the Reagan administration affected African American youths who need to get jobs in small retail firms. African

American youths are particularly affected by a lack of neighborhood retail businesses owned by African Americans.

THE DECLINE IN RELATIVE EARNINGS AMONG AFRICAN AMERICAN YOUTHS IN THE 1980s

During the 1960s and 1970s African Americans made large gains in the labor market relative to whites. Title VII of the 1964 Civil Rights Act, affirmative action programs, and court interpretation of anti-bias laws combined with a tight job market and a consensus to redress historic inequalities helped to increase the level of African Americans in the job market.

African American youth wages and employment are more sensitive to current market realities than those of older workers, whose specific human capital and seniority buffer them from market developments. The racial earnings gap for recent African American labor market entrants widened in the 1980s, especially among college graduates. A racial difference in employment population rates has also widened. The increase in racial earnings gaps among college graduates, where gaps had effectively disappeared in the 1970s, suggests that more was involved than the overall widening of the pay distribution that characterized the 1980s. The widening in the overall distribution could explain why African American workers fared worse relative to white workers.

The increase in differentiation of the post-1970s African American population, regarding the development of a cadre of college graduates and professionals on the one hand and labor force dropouts and the poor on the other, makes the explanation of the decline in the relative employment and earnings of African American youths difficult. The explanation can be attributed to shifts in the relative demand and supply of specific groups combined with weakened employment policy and equal opportunity programs. The economic decline of central city neighborhoods, loss of manufacturing jobs to other regions and overseas, decline in the real minimum wage and the weakening of the union pressure contribute to the change. Increase in crime went hand-in-hand with the unemployment of high school dropouts. Occupational downgrading, due to weakened federal government employment policy and shifting in demand towards the most highly skilled and a large increase in the ratio of African American to white college graduates reduced the relative earnings of African American college graduates. Ronald Taylor concluded in his analysis:

> The Job Training Partnership Act (JTPA), successor to CETA is limited in its ability to meet the special employment-related needs of high-risk youth, given

its current structure, emphasis, and resources. With a minimum of direction or oversight from the federal or state levels, and far fewer resources than those devoted to CETA programs, JTPA-sponsored programs at the local level have been forced to emphasize short-term assistance and rapid placement of participants in such programs have been severely restricted. Only 3 to 5 percent of eligible youths are served by JTPA's current level of resources. Without substantially increased funding, greater programmatic flexibility, and more centralized coordinated activities at the state level, it is unlikely that JTPA will ever become an effective mechanism for providing comprehensive employment and training assistance to high-risk youth most in need of such services.[31]

The 1960s and 1970s were periods of great political, social and economic progress for African Americans as a group. The enactment of the equal opportunity and voting rights laws, the introduction of affirmative action policy, increasing levels of education, and changing attitudes among the general American population—all help to explain the reasons for upward mobility of young African Americans into high-paying professions. These employment trends continued into the 1970s but during the 1980s they were somehow reversed. The Reagan Administration's conservative fiscal policy of budget cut, tax cut and supply-side theory, the weakening of federal enforcement of equal opportunity laws and affirmative action programs explain the reversal in African American employment trends.

NOTES

1. Richard Freeman, "Cutting Black Youth Unemployment," *New York Times* 20 July 1986.
2. National Urban League, *Fact Sheet: The Black Teen Male* (Washington, D.C.: GPO, 1988)
3. James P. Comer, "Poverty, Family, and the Black Experience." in. *Giving Children a Chance: The Case for More Effective National Policies,* ed. G. Miller (Washington, D.C.: Center for National Policy, 1989) 109–130.
4. Lisbeth B. Schorr, *Within Our Reach: Breaking the Cycle of Disadvantage* (New York: Doubleday/Anchor, 1988).
5. Tom E. Larson, *Job Placement of Young Black Males: The Roles of Migration and Structural Change in Urban Labor Market* (Berkeley, California: University of California Press, 1986).
6. James P. Smith and Finis Welch, *Closing the Gap: Forty Years of Economic Progress for Blacks* (Santa Monica, California: Rand Corporation, 1986).
7. Charles A. Murray, *Losing Ground: American Social Policy 1950–1980* (New York: Basic Books, 1986).
8. Irmtraud Seeborg, et al. "Training and Labor Market Outcomes of Disadvantaged Blacks," *Industrial Relations*, Winter, 1986, 25.

9. Kenneth J. Arrow, "The Theory of Discrimination," in *Discrimination in Labor Markets,* ed. A. Pascal (Princeton, NJ: Princeton University Press, 1973).

10. David M. Gordon and others, *Segmented Work, Divided Workers* (Cambridge: Cambridge University Press, 1982).

11. Lester C. Thurow, *Generating Inequality* (New York: Basic Books, 1975).

12. Ray Mey and David Wise, *The Transition from School to Work: The Experience of Blacks and Whites* (Cambridge, Mass.: National Bureau of Economic Research, 1982).

13. U.S. Department of Labor. *Performance results for 107 Job Corps Centers* (Washington, D.C.: Government Printing Office, 1985)

14. Mathematical Policy Research, *Evaluation of the Economic Impact of the Job Corps Program* (Princeton, NJ: Mathematical Policy Research, September, 1982).

15. Charles Betsey and others, *Youth Employment and Training Programs: The YEDPA Years* (Washington, D.C.: National Academy Press, 1985).

16. Robert Mare and Christopher Winship. "The Paradox of Lessening Racial Inequality and Joblessness among Black Youths: Enrollment Enlistment and Employment. 1964–1981," *American Sociological Review* 89, 7 February 1984.

17. Tom Larson, Job Placement of Young Black Males.

18. Larson, Job Placement of Young Black Males.

19. Michael Wachter and C. Kim, "Time Series Changes in Youth Joblessness," Richard Freedman and David Wise, Eds. The Youth Labor Market Problems (Chicago University of Chicago Press, 1982).

20. Larson, Job Placement of Young Black Males.

21. Stanley Lieberson, A Piece of Pie (Berkeley: University of California Press, 1980).

22. Larson, Job Placement of Young Black Males:

23. San Francisco Chronicle, A Rough Day for a Reagan Nominee, San Francisco Chronicle, March 5, 1986.

24. Charles Brown et al., "The Effect of the Minimum Wage on Unemployment." Journal of Economic Literature 20 (June 1982).

25. Daniel P. Moynihan, Ed. On Understanding Poverty: Perspectives from the Social Science (New York: Basic, 1969) 9.

26. Oscar Lewis, "The Culture of Poverty," Daniel Moynihan, ed., On Understanding Poverty: Perspectives from the Social Science (New York: Basic, 1969).

27. Michael Piore, Birds of Passage (Cambridge: Cambridge University Press, 1979).

28. Harvey Hamel, et al. Wage Expectations. Youth Unemployment and Minimum Wages (Washington, D.C.: Bureau of Labor Statistics, 1970).

29. Michael Borus, "Willingness to Work," Michael Borus, ed., Pathways to the Future: A Longitudinal Study of Young Americans (Columbus: Ohio State University, Center for Human Resources Research, 1980).

30. Jerome Culp and Bruce Dunson, "Brothers of a Different Color: A Preliminary Look at Employer Treatment of White and Black Youth," Richard Freeman

and H. Holzer, Eds. The Black Youth Employment Crisis (Chicago: University of Chicago Press, 1986).

31. Ronald T. Taylor, "Improving the Status of Black Youth: Some Lessons from Recent National Experiments," Ronald L. Taylor, ed., African American Youth: Their Social and Economic Status in the United States, (Westport, Conn.: Praeger, 1995) 330.

Chapter Seven

Conclusion

President Ronald Wilson Reagan's conservative ideological fiscal policy had a lasting impact in United States economy. Reagan started his political journey as a Roosevelt liberal democrat. His contact with big business changed his political ideology from liberal to conservative.

His ascendance into the political arena was based on his conservative ideological attack on big government, high taxes, and the federal government deficit. Reagan saw an opportunity in the increasing dissatisfaction with the economic programs that were established by the Democrats. This dissatisfaction and the conservative thrust prompted Reagan to run for national office. His theme was based on the failure of the national economic programs that were supported by Democrats. He criticized the Democratic Party for supporting big government. He blamed the high taxes and the size and costs of government for the country's problems. Liberal policies like aid to low-income families, education, and abortion were also on Reagan's attack list. In 1980, the Jimmy Carter regime was unable to manage the economy, and the Iranian hostage crisis that created more dissatisfaction and lack of confidence in Carter's administration. The election of 1980 propelled Ronald Reagan and his conservative ideology into the presidency.

President Reagan saw his victory as a mandate from the people to change the direction of the national economy. Evidence based on expert analysis of the election suggests that Reagan's victory was not a mandate from the American people to change the economy, but was a vote against Carter due to his inability to manage the national economy and foreign affairs of the United States. Regardless of the accurate, expert analysis of the election outcome, Reagan capitalized on the so-called mandate to further his conservative political ideology and agenda.

As soon as Reagan was elected to office, he made a smart move to solidify his conservative political ideology and agenda in the White House. He took advantage of the political environment to sell his policy agenda to the American people. Reagan immediately selected cabinet members who were deeply rooted in the same conservative political ideology and agenda. These cabinet members were loyal to Reagan and also loyal to the ideological movement. Reagan was the driving force behind this movement and David Stockman, also known, as the axeman was the leader of the pack. The full psychological commitment by these Reaganomics loyalists was the biggest single factor that guaranteed the success of the Reaganomics movement.

Reagan administration's major assault on job programs was launched through the budgetary process. David Stockman, Reagan's budget director, brought several skills with him into the team. Stockman knew how Congress worked, he had a great deal of knowledge of the budgetary process and he was a strong believer in the Reagan conservative fiscal ideology. President Reagan used his political rhetoric and charisma to charm the American people into supporting his programs. He was able to manipulate Congress and silence his critics to the extent that there was no strong opposition to the dismantling of CETA. Reagan saw big government as the barrier to economic problems and he was determined to dismantle what he called the welfare state.

Reagan's campaign promise to balance the federal government's budget and reduce the deficit was not achieved. The federal government budget was not balanced, and the deficit rose to all-time high. The gap between the federal income receipts and expenditure widened, which resulted in a high deficit. Reagan's policy was inconsistent, socially destabilizing, and politically divisive. The basic problem with Reagan's policy was that it overestimated national economic recovery from lower taxes, reduced inflation, balanced budget, increased defense spending, and reduced domestic spending. That was a gross miscalculation. In order to balance the budget, the administration had to balance the difference between the revenues and the expenditures. The administration was robbing Peter to pay Paul by decreasing domestic spending to increase defense spending.

The administration came to a single conclusion that lower tax rates would induce the economy to produce more. A low tax rate would mean that worker's after-tax income would be higher; as a result, more personal disposable income would be created. Consequently, the excess revenue would be utilized for savings and investments. This would eventually translate into high economic growth that would lead to more jobs.

Reagan era was unprecedented in tax and domestic budget cuts. President Reagan's budget policy was characterized by a drastic reduction in domestic programs. Reagan declared a war against the fifty years of Democrat liberal philosophy of taxing and spending. Reagan was also successful in reforming the tax system. During the Reagan decade, several tax revisions and tax codes were passed thus earning the label tax decade.

The administration tax structure focused on tax expenditure measures. This tax process reduced revenues, which consequently widened the gap between tax receipts and tax revenues. The budget cut and tax reform did not stop the growth of the federal government budget deficit. There was huge increase in defense spending, and a significant reduction in domestic social programs. Investments, savings and production did not increase as promised.

Reagan introduced the Job Training Partnership Act to help the economically disadvantaged, but the job program was used to help people who needed it the least. The emphasis in the JTPA was program outcomes. This means that the private contractors were paid based on how many JTPA program participants could be placed in jobs. The federal government's role in JTPA programs was weak. The programs were administered by state and local governments who were given more control to oversee the JTPA programs. Due to the numbers game, which uses numerical standards rather than the characteristics of the population as a measure of performance, JTPA encouraged creaming. Which resulted in selecting those who are more likely to succeed in getting a job even without participating in JTPA; those who are most disadvantaged are left out.

The decade of the 1980s was eventful. Many changes occurred in the national and international arenas. Individual African Americans achieved economic and political success, but as a group, the endeavor of African Americans to gain economic equality was impeded by Reagan fiscal policy. Reagan administration was encouraging the individual achievement of African Americans as the standard for the administration to promote economic equality. The administration's public policy was rooted in a strong conservative political ideology. The theme of Reagan's conservative ideology was based on freedom, order, responsibility, self-help, and laissez-faire, which became the guiding words for promoting equality among African Americans. Consequently, as a group, the African Americans were the biggest losers of this conservative political rhetoric. It is a fact that is clearly echoed by social scientists that the Reagan era was a period when the economic progress of African Americans was stalled. Certainly, there were some variations in economic trends based on region and class. The overall gap in economic equality in the United States is still high. However, some African Americans have gained some economic and political power.

The political, economic and social consequences of unemployment problems are immeasurable. A large percentage of African American youths are at risk and in need. The plight of poor African American youths in the inner cities is a major issue of national debate. In the 1960s and 1970s, the plight of African American youths received a great deal of attention in the national policy, academic, and media arenas. Those decades produced series of federal government policies and programs targeted towards solving the problems of unemployment, poverty, substance abuse, crime and illiteracy among African Americans. The increase in physical and mental health, drug abuse, crime, school dropouts and teenage pregnancy are becoming topics of national interests and debate. Policy makers should refocus their attention on African American youths, because this generation is becoming an endangered species.

African Americans, as a group, experienced a great deal of political, social, and economic progress in the 1960s and 1970s. Certain factors are responsible for the upward mobility of African Americans into higher paying jobs. These factors are: the passage of the equal opportunity and voting rights laws, the establishment of affirmative action policy, increased levels of education, an increase in job programs, and changing attitudes among the general American public. In the 1980s, these trends were somehow reversed. Obviously, the reversal in African American employment trends can be traced to the Reagan administration's conservative fiscal policy of budget cut, tax cut and supply-side theory, and the weakening of federal enforcement of equal opportunity laws and affirmative action programs.

The conclusion of this book suggests that Reagan administration's conservative fiscal policy contributed to the high level of unemployment among African Americans in the 1980s. Through the tax and budget policies, the administration changed employment programs policy. The replacement of the Comprehensive Employment Training Act (CETA) with the Job Training Partnership Act (JTPA) was a major alteration in the employment policy. With JTPA, the emphasis changed from targeting disadvantaged groups to the use of numerical standards without any adjustment for the characteristics of the population the program was serving. This resulted in creaming.

The administration cut stipends for the unemployed, arguing that more people could enroll in job training for less money. More responsibility for federal job training programs was placed at the state government level and in private sector. Employment programs were further altered by deep budget cuts. JTPA was passed by Congress to improve the federal job training programs, but the Reagan administration succeeded in incorporating its political agenda into the new programs. The JTPA reduced the budget authority and provided grants to state and local governments.

Reagan administration's conservative fiscal policy retarded the employment progress that was made by African Americans in the 1960s and 1970s.

The unemployment rate for African Americans increased during the 1980s. The data analysis presented in the book supports the argument that the Reagan administration's conservative fiscal policy was responsible for the high level of unemployment among African Americans.

Reaganomics was not the major cure-all it was promised to be. As a result of the tax reform, revenue declined and the deficit worsened. Unemployment among minorities worsened. No effort was made by the administration against the underlying economic conditions that continued to generate racial inequality in the unemployment rate. The fundamental problem is Reagan administration's failure to create equal labor market outcomes. This book revealed that the persistence of labor market inequality is due to the lack of significant progress in providing African Americans with increased equal opportunity programs. No public effort was made by the administration to change the fundamental economic disadvantages experienced by African Americans. Self-help made it possible for some individuals among African Americans to succeed, but the African American population as a whole made no economic progress.

In the final analysis, the Reagan policy failed because of the lack of cohesive economic policy with full employment as its basic objective. Unfortunately, Reagan's political rhetoric of a new beginning with an economic miracle and trickle-down jobs for all has become, instead, a reality of economic loss for millions of African Americans. The administration's policy of tight money, high interest rates and cuts of federal programs is not what people were promised during the 1980 campaign. Americans were promised economic growth, more jobs, and less inflation.

The differences in unemployment rates between African Americans and whites can be traced to the common practices of the employment selection process rather than to other factors. African Americans are discriminated against in the job market. Other factors pose barriers in the job markets for African Americans such as education, job training and experience. In order for the federal government to address these inequities in the system, a comprehensive policy such as employment and training programs, compensatory education, and anti-discrimination laws would be the appropriate structural approach to assure equal opportunity. Rather, the Reagan administration took liberty in cutting the very programs that would guarantee a labor market without racial discrimination. Such programs would help America achieve equal opportunity and balanced growth.

CETA demonstrated the effectiveness of a targeted federal government employment program. CETA was designed with bipartisan support to provide comprehensive employment policy. It operated through federal grants to over four hundred local and state governments. They were planning and operating employment and training programs to meet local needs. CETA's main objective was to employ and train the economically disadvantaged. Such targeted structural employment programs encouraged the equal employment of minorities and other groups in the labor market. For example, one-third of the participants in CETA's public-service employment Title VI were African Americans. In the 1970s, African Americans make up only two-fifths of the recipients of public housing and school lunches, one third of the 6-million food-stamp recipients, less than one-third of Medicaid recipients and 6 out of every 10 welfare recipients were whites.

African Americans are certainly affected by micro events of which they have no control. The failure of the Reagan administration to develop a full employment policy, the decline of the manufacturing industries, the effect of nepotism, and racial discrimination are not under the control of African Americans. These are not problems that can be solved by the market theory, or increases in education, or self-help political rhetoric but by a comprehensive public policy.

It is a fact that there is a decrease in the range and level of employment opportunities for African American youths in particular. There are fewer jobs for youths in general, in almost all industries with the exception of retail. Due to persistent discrimination, segregation, and nepotism, African American youths are hurting the most. The direct consequence of unemployment can be seen in the high rate of crime, school drop-out, teenage unwed pregnancy, physical and mental health, and substance abuse. These create long lasting economic and social problems and everyone is affected. The high cost of supporting the unproductive and the incarcerated weakens the American economic system. Obviously, given the cost-effectiveness of a viable employment program, the federal government should direct more resources towards full employment. America works when everyone is working.

Bibliography

AFL-CIO, *Daily Proceedings and Executive Council Reports*. Anaheim, California: AFL-CIO, 1985.

——. *The National Economy*. Chicago, Illinois: AFL-CIO, 1986.

——. *The Reagan Budget and Gramm-Rudman-Hollings*. Washington, D.C.: AFL-CIO, 1986.

Alesina, Alberto and Geoffrey Carliner. *Politics and Economies in the Eighties*. Chicago: University of Chicago Press, 1991.

Anderson, Bernard E. and Isabel V. Sawhill. *Youth Employment and Public Policy*. New Jersey: Prentice Hall, Inc. 1980.

Anderson, James E. and others. *Public Policy and Politics in America*. Monterey: Brooks, 1978.

Anderson, Kathryn H. and others. "Mixed Signals in the Job Training Partnership Act". *Growth and Change*. Summer, 1991.

Anderson, Martin. *Revolution: The Reagan Legacy*. Stanford: Hoover Institution Press, 1990.

Anderson, Nels. *The Right to Work*. New York: Modern Age Books, 1938.

Arrow, Kenneth J. "The Theory of Discrimination." In *Discrimination in Labor Markets*, ed. A Pascal. Princeton: Princeton University Press, 1973.

Bailey, Stephen Kemp. *Congress Makes a Law*. New York: Columbia University Press, 1950.

Barnow, Kurt S. and Jill Constantine. *Using Performance Management to Encourage Services to Hard - to - Serve Individuals in JTPA*. Washington, D.C.: National Commission for Employment Policy, 1988.

Barth, James R. and Joseph J. Cordes. "Supply-Side Economics: Political Claims vs. Economic Reality." In *Supply - Side Economics*, eds. Thomas Sau and Paul Masters Carrolton, Georgia: West Georgia College, 1982.

Bartlett Bruce R. *Reaganomics, Supply - Side Economics in Action*. New York: Quill, 1982.

135

Baumer, Donald C. and Carl E. Van Horn. *The Politics of Unemployment*. Washington, D.C.: Congressional Quarterly Press, 1985.

Bowden, Lee and Felicity Skidmore, eds. *Rethinking Employment Policy*. Washington, D.C.: The Urban Institute, 1989.

Berman, Barry. *Looking Back on the Reagan Presidency*. Baltimore, MD: John Hopkins University Press, 1990.

Bernstein Harry. "Labor, Liberals Join Forces to Counter Reagan Agenda." *Los Angeles Times*. 2 September, 1981.

Betsey, Charles, and others. *Youth Employment and Training Programs: The YEDPA Years*. Washington, D.C.: National Academy Press, 1985.

Beveridge, William H. *Full Employment in a Free Society*. London: Allen and Unwin, 1944.

Black, Edwin. "The Second Persona." *Quarterly Journal of Speech*. 56. 1970.

Blaustein, Saul J. *Jobs and Income Security for Unemployment Workers*. Kalamazoo, Michigan: W.E. Upjohn Institute for Employment Research, 1981.

Boris, Michael. "Assessing the Impact of Training Programs." In *Employing the Unemployed*. ed. Eli Ginzberg. New York: Basic Books, 1980.

———. "Willingness to Work." in *Pathways to the Future*: *A Longitudinal Study of Young Americans*. Columbus: Ohio State University, Center for Human Resources Research, 1980.

Boskin, Michael J. *Reagan and the Economy: The Successes, Failures, and Unfinished Agenda*. San Francisco: ICS Press, 1987.

Bound, John and Richard Freeman. "Black Economics Progress: Erosion of the Post-1965 Gains in the 1980s?" In *The Question of Discrimination*. eds. Steven Schulman and William Darity. Middletown, Conn.: Wesleyan University Press, 1989.

———. *What Went Wrong? The Erosion of Relative Earnings and Employment among Young Black Men in the 1980's*. Cambridge, Mass.: NBER, July 1991.

Boyarsky, Bill. *The Rise of Ronald Reagan*. New York: Random House, 1968.

Broder, David. "States Learn to Live with End of New Deal". *The Des Monies Register*, 30 November 1983.

Brown, Charles, and others. "The Effect of the Minimum Wages on Unemployment." *Journal of Economic Literature* June, 1982.

Butler, Stuart, and others. *Mandate for Leadership II*. Washington, D.C.: Heritage Foundation, 1984.

Cannon, Lou. Reagan. New York: G.P. Putnam's Sons, 1982.

Canterbury, Ray E. *The Making of Economics*. Belmont California: Wadsworth, 1978.

Carroll, James D. and others. "Supply-Side Management in the Reagan Administration," *Public Administration Review,* Nov.–Dec. 1985.

Chisman, Forrest. "An Effective Employment Policy: The Missing Middle." In *Rethinking Employment Policy,* eds. Lee Bowden and Felicity Skidmore, Washington D.C.: Urban Institute, 1989.

Citizens for Tax Justice. *Corporate Income Taxes in the Reagan Years*. Washington, D.C.: Citizens for Tax Justice. Oct. 1984.

———. *The Resurgence of Business Investment and Corporate Income Taxes*. Washington, D.C.: Citizens for Tax Justice. Oct. 1986.

Claque, Ewan, and Leo Kramer. *Manpower Policies and Programs A Review*, 1935–1975. Kalamazoo: W.E. Upjohn Institute for Employment Research, 1976.

Comer, James P. "Poverty, Family, and Black Experience." In *Given Children a Chance: The Case for More Effective National Policies*. Washington, D.C.: Center for National Policy, 1989.

Congressional Black Caucus. *Quality of Life, Fiscal 1990 Alternative Budget*. Washington, D.C.: Congressional Black Caucus, 1989.

Conlan, Timothy. New Federalism: *Intergovernmental Reform from Nixon to Reagan*. Washington D.C.: Brookings, 1988.

Craypo, Charles. "The Decline in Union Bargaining Power." In *U.S. Labor Relations 1945–1989: Accommodation and Conflict*. New York: Garland Publishing, 1990.

Culp, Jerome and Bruce Dunson. "Brothers of a Different Color: A Preliminary Look of Employer Treatment of White and Black Youth." In *The Black Youth Employment Crisis. Chicago:* University of Chicago Press, 1986.

Dalleck, Robert. *Ronald Reagan*. Cambridge: Harvard University Press. 1984.

Dane, Francis C. *Research Methods*. Pacific Grove, CA: Brooks, 1990.

Darity, William and Samuel Myers. "Distress v. Dependency: Changing Income Support Programs." *The Urban League Review*, Winter 1986–87.

Davidson, Roger H. *The Politics of Comprehensive Manpower Reform*. Baltimore, MD: John Hopkins University Press, 1972.

Dement, E.F. "North Carolina Balance of State: Decentralization and Discontinuity." In *The T in CETA*. Eds. Sar A. Levitan and G. L. Mangum Kalamazoo: Upjohn Institute, 1981.

Eastman, Karen R. "Local Liability and CETA: Is the Price too High?" *County Employment Reporter.* December 1980.

Easton, David. *The Political System: An Inquiry into the State of Political Science*. Chicago: University of Chicago Press, 1981.

———. *A System Analysis of Political Life*. New York: Wiley, 1965.

Ehrenberg, Ronald G. and Robert S. Smith. *Modern Labor Economics: Theory and Public Policy*. New York: Scott, Foresman and Co. 1985.

Ellwood, John. "Controlling the Growth of Federal Domestic Spending." In *Reductions in U.S. Domestic Spending,* ed. John Ellwood. New Brunswick: Transaction Books, 1982.

Flaim, Paul O. "The Effect of Demographic Changes on the Nation's Unemployment Rate." *Monthly Labor Review*, March 1979.

Foner, Fillip. *Organized Labor and the Black Worker*. New York: International Publishers, 1981.

Franklin, Grace A. and Randall B. Ripley. *CETA: Politics and Policy, 1973–1982*. Knoxville: University of Tennessee Press, 1984.

Freeman, Richard. "Cutting Black Youth Unemployment," *New York Times*. 20 July 1986.

Friedlander, Stanley L. *Unemployment in the Urban Core*. New York: Praeger, 1972.

Fusfeld, Daniel R. *The Age of the Economist*, Glenview, Illinois: Scott, Foresman, 1966.

138   *Bibliography*

Galbraith, John Kenneth and Paul W. McCracken. *Reaganomics: Meaning Means, and Ends*. New York: Free Press, 1983.

Garraty, John A. *Unemployment in History*. New York: Harper and Row, 1978.

Ginsburg, Helen. *Full Employment and Public Policy: The United States and Sweden*. Toronto: Lexington, 1983.

Glazer, Nathan. "The Social Policy of the Reagan Administration." In *The Social Contract Revisited*, ed. Lee Bowden. Washington, D.C.: Urban Institute, 1984.

Goldfield, Michael. *The Decline of Organized Labor in the United States*. Chicago: University of Chicago Press, 1987.

Goodsell, Charles T. *The Case for Bureaucracy*. Chatham, NJ: Chatham House, 1994.

Gordon, David M. *Theories of Poverty and Unemployment: Orthodox, Radical and Dual Labor Market Perspectives*. Lexington: Lexington Books, 1972.

———. *Segmented Work, Divided Workers*. Cambridge: Cambridge University Press, 1982.

Gorham, William. "Overview." In *The Social Contract Revisited*. Washington, D.C.: Urban Institute Press, 1984.

Granvelle, Jane G. *Tax Subsides for Investment: Issues and Proposals*. Washington, D.C.: Library of Congress, 92-2055, Feb. 1992.

Hailstones, Thomas J. A. *Guide to Supply-Side Economics*. Reston, VA: Reston Publishing Co., 1982.

Hamel, Harvey and others. *Wage Expectations: Youth Unemployment and Minimum Wages*. Washington, D.C.: Bureau of Labor Statistics, 1970.

Hector, Hugh and Rudolph G. Penner. "Fiscal and Political Strategy in the Reagan Administration." In *The Reagan Presidency: An Early Assessment*, ed. Fred Greenstein. Baltimore: The John Hopkins University Press, 1983.

Heilbroner, Robert L. *The Worldly Philosophers*. New York: Simon and Schuster, 1977.

Henderson, Lenneal. "Budget, Taxes, and Politics: Options for the African American Community." *The State of Black America*, 1991.

———. "Budget and Tax Strategy Implications for Blacks." *The State of Black America*, 1990.

Herbers, John. "The New Federalism: Unplanned, Innovative and Here to Stay." *Governing,* May 1985.

———. "President Asserts Economic Policies Prove Effective." *New York Times*, 14 October, 1982.

Hofstadter, Richard. *The Paranoid Style in American Politics*. New York: Alfred A. Knopt, 1981.

Howe, Wayne J. "Education and Demographics: How Do They Affect Unemployment Rates?" *Monthly Labor Review*, January 1988.

Jennings, James. *Race, Politics and Economic Development*. New York: Verso, 1992.

Jennings, Kent and Thomas Mann, eds. *Elections at Home and Abroad: Essays in Honor of Warren E. Miller.* Ann Arbor: University of Michigan, 1994.

Johnson, George E. "Do We Know Enough about the Unemployment Problem to Know What, If Anything, will Help?" In *Rethinking Employment Policy,* ed., Lee Bowden. Washington, D.C.: Urban Institute, 1989.

Johnston, Janet W. *The Job Training Partnership Act: A Report by the National Commission for Employment Policy.* Washington, D.C.: GPO, 1987.

Jones, Charles O. *An Introduction to the Study of Public Policy.* Monterey, CA: Brooks, 1984.

———. *The Reagan Legacy: Promise and Performance.* Chatham: Chatham House, 1988.

Kearl, James and other, "A Confusion of Economists?" *American Economic Review.* May 1979.

Keisling, Phil, "Reform Jobless Benefits," *New York Times.* 23 January 1983.

Keleher, Robert E. "The Theoretical Basis and Historical Origins of Supply-Side Economics." In *Supply-Side Economics: Pro and Con*, eds. G. Thomas Sav and Paul E. Masters. Carrolton: West Georgia College, 1982.

Keynes, John Maynard. *The General Theory of Employment, Interest and Money.* New York: Harcourt, Brace & Co., 1936.

Kiewe, Amos and Davis W. Houck. *A Shining City on a Hill.* New York: Praeger, 1991.

Kimzey, Bruce W. *Reaganomics.* New York: West Publishing Co., 1983.

Kirschton, Dick. "Decision-Making in the White House: How Well Does It Serve the President?" *National Journal*, April 1982.

Kondracke, Morton, "Reagan's I. Q." *The New Republic*, 24 March, 1982.

Kozhimannil, T. Varghese. *The Reagan Presidency: Promises and Performances.* New York: Cimothas, 1989.

Kozol, Jonathan. *Illiterate America.* New York: Doubleday, 1985.

Krashevski, Richard S. "What is Full Employment?" *Challenge.* November–December, 1986.

Kristol, Irving. "Toward a New Economics?" *Wall Street Journal.* 9 May 1977.

Larson, Tom E. *Job Placement of Young Black Males: The Roles of Migration and Structural Change in Urban Labor Market.* Berkeley: University of California Press, 1986.

Leuchtenburg, William. "Ronald Reagan's Liberal Post," *The New Republic*, 23 May 1983.

Levitan, Sar A., and others. *Human Resources and Labor Markets.* New York: Harper and Row, 1981.

Lewis, Oscar. "The Culture of Poverty." In *An Understanding Poverty: Perspectives from the Social Science*, ed, Daniel Moynihan. New York: Basic, 1969.

Lieberson, Stanley. *A Piece of Pie.* Berkeley: University of California Press, 1980.

Light, Paul. *The President's Agenda: Domestic Policy Choice from Kennedy to Carter.* Baltimore: The John Hopkins University Press, 1982.

Lincoln Institute. *Labor Policy, Minorities and Youths.* Washington, D.C.: Lincoln Institute, 1983.

Lowe, Carl. *Reaganomics: The New Federalism.* New York; H.W. Wilson Co. 1984.

MacMahon, Arthur, and others. *The Administration of Federal Work Relief.* Chicago: Public Administration Service, 1941.

Mangum, Garth. *MDTA: The Foundation of Federal Manpower Policy.* Baltimore, MD: John Hopkins University Press, 1968.

Mare, Robert and Christopher Winship. "The Paradox of Lessening Racial Inequality and Joblessness among Black Youths: Enrollment Enlistment and Employment. 1964–1981" *American Sociological Review*. 7 February 1984.

Marshall, Ray. "Selective Employment Programs and Economics Policy." *Journal of Economic Issues*. March 1984.

McBurney, Donald H. Research Methods. Pacific Grove, CA: Brooks, 1994.

Mey, Ray and David Wise, *The Transition from School to Work: The Experience of Blacks and Whites*. Cambridge: National Bureau of Economic Research, 1982.

Meyer, Laurence H. *The Supply - Side Effects of Economic Policy*. Boston: Kluwer Publishing, 1981.

Mikesell, John L. *Fiscal Administration: Analysis and Applications for the Public Sector*. Chicago, IL: The Dorsey Press, 1986.

Miller, Warren E. "The Election of 1984 and the Future of American Politics," In *Elections in America*, ed. Kay L. Schlozman. Boston: Allen & Unwin, 1987.

Mirengoff, William, et al. *CETA: Accomplishments, Problems, Solutions*. Kalamazoo, MI: Upjohn Institute, 1982.

Mitchell, Broadus. *Depression Decade: The Economic History of the United States*. New York: Holt, Rinehart and Winston, 1947.

Mitchell, Daniel and John M. Olin. *An Action Plan to Create Jobs*. Washington, D.C.: Heritage Foundation, 1992.

Moynihan, Daniel P., ed. *On Understanding Poverty: Perspectives from the Social Science*. New York: Basic, 1969.

Muir, William Ker. The Bully Pulpit: *The Presidential Leadership of Ronald Reagan*. San Francisco: Institute for Contemporary Studies, 1992.

Murray, Charles. *Losing Ground: American Social Policy 1950–1980*. New York: Basic Books, 1986.

Musgrave, Richard A. "The Reagan Administration's Fiscal Policy." In *Reaganomics*, eds. W. Craig Subblebine and Thomas D. Willet. San Francisco: ICS Press, 1983.

Nathan, Richard, and others. *The Consequence of Cuts: The Effects of the Reagan Domestic Program on State and Local Governments*. Princeton: Princeton Urban and Regional Research Center, 1983.

National Urban League. *Black Americans and Public Policy*. Washington, D.C.: National Urban League, 1988.

Nelson, Jack. "The Reagan Legacy." In *Beyond Reagan: The Politics of Upheaval*, ed. Paul Duke. New York: Warner Books, 1986.

Neustadt, Richard E. *Presidential Power and Modern Presidents: The Politics of Leadership from Roosevelt to Reagan*. New York: Free Press, 1990.

Niskanem, William A. Reaganomics: *An Insider's Account of the Policies and the People*. New York: Oxford University Press, 1988.

Oates, Wallace. *Fiscal Federalism*. New York: Harcourt, Brace & Jovanovich, 1972.

Ornstein, Norman J., and Shirley Elder. *Interests Groups, Lobbying and Policymaking*. Washington, D.C.: Congressional Press, 1978.

Palmer, John L., and Isabel Sawhill, eds. *The Reagan Experiment: An Examination of Economic and Social Policies under Reagan Administration*. Washington, D.C.: Urban Institute, 1982.

Patterson, Bradley H. *The King of Power*. New York: Basic Books, 1988.

Phillips, Kevin. *The Politics of Rich and Poor: Wealth and the American Electorate in the Reagan Aftermath*. New York: Random House, 1990.

Pierson, Frank C. *The Minimum Level of Unemployment and Public Policy*. Kalamazoo, Michigan: Upjohn, 1980.

Pigou, Arthur C. *Theory of Unemployment*. London: Frank Cass and Co. 1933.

Piore, Michael. *Birds of Passage*. Cambridge: Cambridge University Press, 1979.

Rashkin, Ilona. *Dealing with Fraud and Abuse under the Comprehensive Employment Training Act*. Washington, D.C.: Congressional Research Service, 1981.

Rauch, Jonathan. "Stockman's Quiet Revolution of OMB Mary Leave Indelible Mark on Agency." *National Journal*, 25 May 1985.

Reagan, Ronald and Richard G. Hubler. *Where's the Rest of Me?* New York: Duell, Sloan and Pearce, 1965.

Ripley, Randall B. and Grace A Franklin. "The Private Sector in Public Employment and Training Programs." *Policy Studies Review*. 2 May 1983.

Ritter, Kurt and David Henry. *Ronald Reagan: The Great Communicator*. New York: Greenwood, 1992.

Rissman, Ellen R. "What is the Natural Rate of Unemployment?" *Economic Perspective*. Chicago: Federal Reserve Bank, Oct/Nov 1986.

Rourke, Francis. "Executive Responsiveness to Presidential Policies: The Reagan Presidency." *Congress and the Presidency*. Spring 1990.

Rowan, Carl. "Reagan's Budget Forces Us Anew to Debate Federal Role," *Chicago Sun-Times*, February 1986.

Ruthenberg, Stanley H. and Jocelyn Cutchess. *Manpower Challenge of the 1970's*. Baltimore: John Hopkins University Press, 1970.

Solru, Anondi P. and Ronald L. Tracy, eds. *The Economic Legacy of the Reagan Years: Euphoria or Chaos*. New York: Praeger, 1991.

Salomon, Lester M. and Alan J. Abramson. "Governance." In *The Assessment of America's Changing Domestic Priorities*, eds John L. Palmer and Isabel Sawhill. Washington, D.C.: Urban Institute, 1984.

Sargent, Jon. "An Improving Job Market for College Graduates: 1986 Update of Projection to 1995." *Occupational Outlook Quarterly*, Summer 1986.

Sawyer, James E. *Why Reaganomics and Keynesian Economic Failed*. New York: St. Martin's Press, 1987.

Say, Jean Baptiste. "A Treatise on Political Economy." In *The Critics of Keynesian Economics*, ed. Henry Hazlitt. Princeton: Van Nostrand, 1960.

Schorr, Lisbeth B. *Within Our Reach: Breaking the Cycle of Disadvantage*. New York: Doubleday/Anchor, 1988.

Schumpeter, Joseph. *History of Economic Analysis*. New York: Oxford University Press, 1954.

Shannon, John. "The Return to Fend-for-Yourself Federalism: The Reagan Mark." *Intergovernmental Perspective*. Summer/Fall 1987.

Slagle, Frank J. "A Decade of Tax Policy: A Reflection of the Economic Dilemmas and Budget Deficit during the 1980's," *New England Law Review*. Fall 1990.

Smith, Adam. *The Wealth of Nations*. New York: Random House, 1937.

Bibliography

Smith, James P. and Finis Welch. *Closing the Gap: Forty Years of Economic Progress for Blacks*. Santa Monica: Rand Corporation, 1986.

Solow, Robert M. "Solow, On Theory of Unemployment." *The American Economic Review*, 1980.

Sowell, Thomas. "Adam Smith in Theory and Practice." In *Adam Smith and Modern Political Economy*, ed. Gerald P. O'Driscall. Ames, IA: Iowa State University Press, 1979.

Steuerle, Eugene. *The Tax Decade*. Washington, D.C.: The Urban Institute Press 1992.

Stewart, Charles H. "The Politics of Tax Reform in the 1980's." In *Politics and Economics in the Eighties,* eds. Alberto Alesina and Geoffrey Carliner. Chicago: University of Chicago Press, 1991.

Stockman, David. *The Triumph of Politics*. New York: Harper & Row, 1986.

Sandquist, James L. *Politics and Policy*. Washington, D.C.: Brookings Institute, 1968.

Taylor, Ronald T., ed. *African American Youth: Their Social and Economic Status in the United States*. Westport, CT: Praeger, 1995.

Thurow, Lester C. *Generating Inequality*. New York: Basic Books, 1975.

Treiman, Donald J. et al. *Woman, Work and Wages: Equal Pay for Jobs of Equal Value*. Washington, D.C.: National Academy Press, 1981.

U.S. Advisory Commission on Intergovernmental Relations. *Reducing Unemployment: Intergovernmental Dimensions of a National Problem*. Washington, D.C.: Advisory Commission on Intergovernmental Relations, 1982.

U.S. Bureau of Labor Statistics. *Handbook of Labor Statistics*. Washington, D.C.: Bureau of Labor Statistics, 1980.

U.S. Congress. *Congressional Record*. Washington, D.C.: U.S. Government Printing Office, 1980.

U.S. Congress House Committee on Education and Labor. *Compilation of Selected Federal Legislation Relating to Employment and Training*. Washington, D.C.: U.S. Government Printing Office, 1980.

U.S. Congress. Congressional Budget Office. *Temporary Measures to Stimulate Employment: An Evaluation of Some Alternatives*. Washington, D.C.: Congressional Budget Office, 1979.

U.S. Department of Labor. *Employment and Training Report of the President*. Washington, D.C.: Department of Labor, 1980.

U.S. Department of Labor. *Budget FY 1981*. Washington, D.C.: U.S. Government Printing Office, January 1980.

U.S. Executive Office of the President, Office of Management and Budget. *Budget of the United States Government FY 1981*. Washington, D.C.: U.S. Government Printing Office, 1981.

———. *Economic Report of the President*. Washington, D.C.: U.S. Government Printing Office, 1982.

Vedder, Richard K. *Out of Work is Government the Major Cause of Unemployment?* Washington, D.C.: Heritage Foundation, 1993.

Victor, Kirk. "Helping the Haves," *National Journal,* 14 April 1990.

Wachter, Michael and C. Kim. "Time Series Changes in Youth Joblessness." In *The Youth Labor Market Problems*, eds. Richard Freedman and David Wise. Chicago: University of Chicago Press, 1982.

Warshaw, Shirley Anne. "White House Control of Domestic Policy Making: The Reagan Years." *Public Administration Review*, May–June 1995.

Wildavsky, Aaron. *The Politics of the Budgetary Process*. Boston: Little, Brown and Co., 1974.

Wise, Loise R. *Labor Market Policies and Employment Patterns in the United States*. Boulder: Westview Press, 1985.

Welch, Finis. "Black-White Differences in Returns to Education." *American Economic Review*, December 1973.

Index